Rock

ARCHIVES

MICHAEL OCHS

Rock

ARCHIVES

A Photographic Journey

Through the First Two Decades

Of Rock & Roll

~//~

Introduction by Peter Guralnick

Design by Vincent Winter

A DOLPHIN BOOK

DOUBLEDAY & COMPANY, INC. *Garden City, New York*

This is dedicated to the ones I love

A Sarah Lazin Book

Copyright © 1984 by Michael Ochs
All Rights Reserved
PRINTED IN THE UNITED STATES OF AMERICA

First Edition

"Whole Lot Of Shakin' Going On" by Dave Williams and Sunny David.
Copyright © 1957, by Do-Viea Music Co. and Marilyn Music.
"High School Confidential" by Jerry Lee Lewis and Ron Hargrove.
Copyright © 1957, by Penron Music Publishing.   "That Is Rock & Roll"
by Jerry Leiber and Mike Stoller. Copyright © 1959, by Chappell Music,
Bienstock and Quintet Music.   "Rock and Roll Is Here to Stay" by David
White. Copyright © 1958, by Golden Egg Music and Singular Music.

Library of Congress Cataloging in Publication Data

ROCK ARCHIVES.
    Includes index.
    1. Rock music—United States—Pictorial works.   2. Rock musicians—
Portraits.
I. Ochs, Michael.   ML3534.R6   1984   784.5'4'00973   84-4063
ISBN 0-385-19433-1
ISBN 0-385-19434-X (pbk.)

CONTENTS

PREFACE

ITH THE INCREASING POPULARITY of rock videos and books, rock & roll music has become more of an audio-visual form than ever before. The musical high is basically an aural experience, but it can be augmented and expanded by concerts, fan magazines, or, would you believe, a Woodstock Nation?

Danny and the Juniors were right when they sang, "Rock & roll will never die, it was meant to be / It'll go down in history, just you wait and see." I witnessed rock's birth. I listened to Alan Freed on the radio and I went to his live shows at the New York Paramount Theatre, where I saw Jackie Wilson, Buddy Holly and Clyde McPhatter live, something not possible today. From Sha Na Na to the Stray Cats, from all the tributes to the thefts, rock & roll's past and its practitioners will never rest in peace. The trends come and go—they always have and they always will. But rock itself will not die. To further ensure rock & roll's immortality, ROCK ARCHIVES was created. This is the first time so many ghosts from the past have appeared in one place at one time for one price.

The greatest thing about popular music—and rock & roll in particular—is that it's one of the most immediate forms of communication within the culture. A record, like a photograph, is an instant encapsulation of time and the means by which that time can be shared with others at a later date. Yet because many contemporary writers and fans are enamored of a particular time—say, the Fab '50s or the Mod '60s—they can only express in words ideas meant to convince the rest of us how great that time and its music must have been. Only your own personal experience can allow you to feel respect for those whose work comes alive every single time you hear a song. With ROCK ARCHIVES I've sought to present a vast, though incomplete and admittedly subjective, collection of photographs from many eras, the visual complement to countless sounds.

Though the music is paramount, photographs add a priceless dimension. Except for the biggest stars, the artists themselves traditionally have been very transient. Perhaps they underestimated their own importance and so neglected to save records and pictures; maybe they just didn't care. At any rate, they are gone. And since the music business is a business first, the artists—and the history—remain at the mercy of whatever is economically feasible. Storage and upkeep all demand time, money and care. As with most arts, there is rarely sufficient appreciation for the past. But music is cyclical: "Train Kept A-Rollin'" was written by and a hit for Tiny Bradshaw in the '40s, made a hit by the Burnettes' Rock 'n' Roll Trio in the '50s, resurrected in the '60s by the Yardbirds and returned a decade after that, courtesy of Aerosmith. A great song, sound or style can always be resurrected and reshaped.

Unlike most collectors, I don't preserve the rarity of a photograph by keeping it out of circulation. I want anyone who can appreciate a rare shot of Wilbert Harrison to have a chance to see it. When you heard "Kansas City," you had to wonder, "Was that singer as cocky as he sounded?" And if you look on page 121, you'll see Harrison with a strutting look on his face and a gold and diamond guitar-shaped pin on his lapel—everything you hoped he would be. For the most part, we expect the visual images to live up to our aural fantasies and the photographs did just that—in some cases, technically aided by the perfect lighting, makeup and sometimes retouching. But who wants an overweight, acned teen idol anyway?

Though I tried to include as many musical greats as I could, space limitations and unavailable or nonexistent photos led to many omissions. My apologies to all those artists not represented here and my appreciation for all those who are. From Johnny Ace to Mrs. Miller, you were all there making music and making our lives more enjoyable. In my life, music has been the only marriageable mistress I've found. May you enjoy this book as much as I've enjoyed the twenty-five years of collecting these photos and facts.

I WOULD ESPECIALLY LIKE to thank the following people for contributing time, photos and anything else that helped shape this book: Mary Aldin, Brooks Arthur, Alan Betrock, Pat Britt, Harold Bronson, Ted Carroll, Les Cauchi, Alan Clarke, Paul Colby, Bobbi Cowan, Joe Daigle, Spencer Davis, Henry Diltz, Jimmy Evans, Ray Funk, Jonathan and Ronnie Greenfield, Peter Guralnick, Ersel Hickey, Tom and Michelle Hickey, Richard Hite, Jerry Hopkins, Bones Howe, Peter Kanze, Johnny Keyes, James J. Kriegsmann, Jr., Thomas Kriegsmann, Grelun Landon, Brenda Lee, Allan Mason, Huey Meaux, Arthur C. Mensor, Bob Merlis, Alice Ochs, Jim O'Neal, Johnny Otis, Don Paulsen, Bonnie Peterson, Steve Petryszyn, Richard Reicheg, Alan Rinde, Mike Settle, Dominic Sicilia, John and Shelby Singleton, Nik Venet, Billy Vera, Alan Warner, Dick Waterman and Randy Wood.

Special thanks to James Kriegsmann, Sr., who was there before rock was history and is still there for historians like me. And to all of the unknown photographers who captured and expanded our rock dreams.

For their help in the production of this book, I would like to thank: Philip Bashe, Doug Bergstresser, Trent Duffy, Stephanie Franklin, Holly George, Nancy Inglis, Brant Mewborn and Ed Sturmer.

Thanks to Sarah Lazin for believing there was a worthwhile book within the Archives, and to Jim Fitzgerald, who believed Sarah. Special thanks to Vincent Winter, who gave up a promising ice skating career to design this book, smiling all the while. And to his cohorts, wife Martine Winter, Nancy Eising, Barbara Huhn and Ann Pomeroy. Patty Romanowski kept me concise, Lynne Richardson kept me on track through thick and thin, Wendy G. kept me on the edge. And we all kept our sense of humor.

—MICHAEL OCHS

INTRODUCTION

~~~~~~

by Peter Guralnick

I MAGES INFORM our every thought. Long after precise memories have faded, long after we have forgotten intricacies of plot or the daunting weave of history, often a single vivid image will remain. Sometimes, like a half-remembered childhood dream, it cries for explanation. Frequently it distorts the full-focus picture, zooming in on some otherwise indistinguishable detail and assigning to it inexplicable primacy. Occasionally it will illuminate a world.

Rock & roll, pop culture in general, is a collection of moments. It is easy to blow these moments out of proportion—like album snapshots they can be as eloquent or as unyielding as personal memory and mythology allow, serving private icono-graphic needs and entering into the collective unconscious at one and the same time. What memories does a song evoke? Sharp images of personal experience mingle with the inchoate yearnings of a generation. Where were you when you heard the news of John F. Kennedy/John Lennon/Elvis Presley's death?

It's the same with pictures. There simply is no denying the youthful vibrancy not just of the music but of the *image* of a twenty-year-old Elvis Presley, heavy-lidded, insouciant, bursting with energy, as full of edgy confidence in his stance as in his music. Or, conversely, who can put out of mind the sad shots of Elvis at the end, the painful contrast not just in the physical weight but in the *aura* he had to drag around? Or the indelible image of a Janis Joplin sprawled on a broken backstage sofa in her spangled party dress, an ankle bracelet on her leg and a bottle of Southern Comfort clutched in her hand? "You say that music's for the birds," sang the Coasters. "You can't understand the words / Well, honey, if you did / You'd really blow your lid / Baby, that is rock & roll."

There are lots of images and sounds that encapsulate rock & roll for all of us. I don't remember much about Elvis myself pre–"Heartbreak Hotel," but I remember the first time I heard Little Richard certainly—"A-wop-bop-alu-bop-a-wop-bam-boom"—those were the words, and I don't know that I understood *them* at the time. Cinematic images loop in my mind: Elvis dying in *Love Me Tender*; Jerry Lee Lewis making his customary grand entrance, on the back of a flatbed truck in this particular instance, and singing, "Open up, honey, it's your loverboy, me, that's a-knocking" at the outset of *High School Confidential*; and, of course, Gene Vincent with the Blue Caps flipping off their little blue caps in the classic *The Girl Can't Help It*.

These are childhood memories reinforced by an adopted cosmogony, but it was a picture that I saw much later, on publication of the first edition of *The Rolling Stone Illustrated History of Rock & Roll* in 1976, that lent ironic distance and depth, some counterpoint to my memories. The frontispiece to the *Rolling Stone* volume presented a portrait of a singer named Ersel Hickey (one hit, Number 75 on the pop charts in 1958, the occasionally revived "Bluebirds over the Mountain"). The photograph was taken by Gene LaVerne of Buffalo, New York—this was the signature logo in the lower right-hand corner—probably at the moment of Hickey's greatest fame. Take a look at the improbably sculpted helmet of hair, the tommy-gun guitar stance, the pleated pants, cocked leg, patent leather casual footwear and turned-up collar. But somehow there is more to the picture than this. Guitar pick poised, background airbrushed out, every fold of clothing carefully arranged, there is a wistful note being struck. Ersel Hickey seems caught somehow, trapped in a limbo where his cheekbones will forever be accentuated, his thoughts inscrutable, his respectability in doubt (he seems somehow neither a convincing teen idol nor a fully accredited rebel), his gaze forever fixed on a point in the middle distance—the future perhaps?—which he regards unsmilingly but with some measure of hope. It is only a publicity picture, I tell myself, aimed at doing no more than showing Ersel Hickey in the best light. But what volumes it speaks of aspiration and style, fate and fantasy, revelation in artifice. It is in effect a self-portrait of rock & roll.

THERE'S A STORY connected to this picture. Twenty-five years after it was taken, Michael Ochs—who through the eponymous Michael Ochs Archives had supplied *Rolling Stone* with the picture in the first place—got a call at home in California. It was Ersel Hickey. Michael, who by now had been in the business of dream substantiation for over a decade, blanched a little, because this was the first photo subject he had ever heard from. But Hickey wanted only to say thanks. Publication of the picture had opened up a whole new career for the one-time rockabilly who, it turned out, was a native of Buffalo presently living in New Jersey. When Hickey suggested getting together to say thank you in person, Ochs, who was traveling back and forth cross-country to put together this book, said they could meet in New York. Why not James Kriegsmann's studio? Hickey suggested, since he had to pick up some publicity photos there anyway. "James junior?" asked Michael, who had disseminated a number of Kriegsmann's vintage photos of the rock era, the Sinatra era, the Cotton Club era and beyond. No. James senior was still around, same place, same location, right off of Times Square.

When he entered Kriegsmann's studio, Ochs says, it was as if he had died and gone to heaven. Not only was the seventy-four-year-old Kriegsmann still in business, with a busy crew shooting stars, showgirls and acts that walked in off the street; the studio itself—entered via a broad spiral staircase that winds down from a street-level reception area—was like the robbers' cave in the story of Ali Baba and the forty thieves, an unsuspected subterranean fantasy world, still set up like the '40s nightclub/restaurant it once was. There was a wet bar in one corner, wrought-iron circular tables, three spacious areas for shooting, darkrooms, copiers, facilities to turn out an astonishing volume of prints, and of course pictures, pictures (Adam Clayton Powell, the very young Frank Sinatra, Cab Calloway, the Andrews Sisters, a fifteen-year-old Paul Anka) all around. Thus the Michael Ochs Archives expanded into new territory. A book that already had over a thousand photographs (worth how many words?) was recast yet again at the eleventh hour, and Michael Ochs set his prodigious verbal talents to work ("People hearing his rapid-fire speech," wrote journalist Ed Ward of Michael, "have assumed [fallaciously] he was hooked on amphetamines") to convince Kriegsmann, a worldly Viennese emigré who also happens to be the author of Dave "Baby" Cortez's "The Happy Organ" as well as some twenty-five other recorded compositions, that he was the man who could make money out of the detritus of history, that he knew the value of Kriegsmann's back files even if Kriegsmann didn't, that they should go into business together. Needless to say, he succeeded.

That is the way the Michael Ochs Archives has been put together: through a combination of love, greed, fast talk and just plain luck. Michael Ochs refers to himself with equal seriousness as a cultural custodian and a junk collector "regurgitating" the past, and he is perfectly content with either assessment. What is there to say, after all, about a shot of Big Mama Thornton singing "Hound Dog" that reveals after not a great deal of scrutiny a pair of trousered legs protruding from beneath her widespread stance? Is that the glory of rock & roll? Well, if you have a sense of absurdity, maybe it is. Or what could suggest as succinctly both the ambition and acrobatic grace of a singer like Jackie Wilson, who is pictured circa 1951 in his earlier incarnation as a boxer with glowering eyebrows, abundant chest hair and trunks imprinted with the insignia "G&S Sporting Goods"? Nat "King" Cole with a cigarette holder and checkered hat, an eight-year-old Gladys Knight standing on a box to reach the mike on *The Ted Mack Original Amateur Hour*, Paul Simon fronting an early group, Tico and the Triumphs—where else could you find a picture of Billy Lee Riley and the Little Green Men (the group's name dated from Riley's 1957 near-hit, "Flyin' Saucers Rock 'n' Roll"), even if the polite black-and-white photograph shows little evidence of their unusual pigmentation? If you're the kind of person who worries about when Ricky Nelson changed his name to Rick, you will no doubt note that young Ricky's various inlaid and embossed guitars all carry the more "adult" shortened signature. T-Bone Walker doing a split while playing the guitar behind his head foreshadows Chuck Berry, Bo Diddley, and by extension Elvis Presley, who took much of his early stage manner from observing

Bo's performance at the Apollo. James Brown backstage at the Apollo, relaxed, barechested, but still looking as if he is coiled to spring, recalls the epic grandeur of his '60s shows, and Sam Cooke and a young Cassius Clay together are rare partners in grace and self-promotion.

Michael Ochs could discourse to you for hours on these subjects and on such diverse topics as period makeup, highlighting to bring out skin tones, the transformation of the process in black hairstyling, the period authenticity of various microphones, the play of light and dark on a subject's face. What informs this collection of photographs is his passion for such detail, his undifferentiated avidity for the pursuit of the never-before-seen or -heard and his cheerful acceptance of the absurdity of the quest. That is what makes this book so different, I think, from the standard random selection: both the comprehensiveness of Michael's knowledge on the one hand and the uniqueness of his point of view on the other. It is not so much the presence alone of so many authentic originals (black groups you only heard once, rockabillies you never even heard of) as their presentation in a context of reverential irony. What distinguishes Michael's approach from the ordinary run of obsessive/compulsive collector behavior is the spirit of eccentricity that goes with it, the anarchic impulse unstilled, the willful insistence on the fundamental craziness of rock & roll. It's Michael Ochs's ambition to encapsulate "all the spontaneity, sexuality and creativity that [first] drew youth to the power and possibilities of rock & roll." Well, that's a tall order, and I don't know if any collection can quite fill the bill, but ROCK ARCHIVES certainly tries. Even as the book is going to press, the search for the perfect photograph continues, as Michael flies frantically about the country on the rumor that rare early shots of Paul Simon have surfaced or the Little Green Men have landed or a legendary photographer's files, long thought to have been lost, have turned up in storage in Anchorage, Alaska. This is a detective story without an ending, the kind of fantasy quest that we all have imagined as children, only it's even better in real life. Michael's work is a labor of love—and the love shows through on every page.

I HAVE OFTEN WISHED that I had taken a camera with me on some of my own jaunts into history. I wish that I could have captured on film some of the rare moments that I have observed: Muddy Waters at home; Jerry Lee Lewis puffing a cigar in the back seat of a white Lincoln convertible that was pulling a trailer with a solitary piano on it; Bo Diddley, the Duchess and Jerome acting up onstage; Merle Haggard at the Jimmie Rodgers Memorial Festival in Meridian, Mississippi; Solomon Burke in church. I think what inhibited me from taking the camera, in addition to an irrational mistrust of the mechanical, was my fear that I would miss the moment in seeking to capture it; that simply by adding one more cumbersome piece of paraphernalia (tape recorder, notebook, pencil, camera, reporter) I would spook reality, deny process and prevent whatever it was that might be happening from happening. Well, ROCK ARCHIVES gives me back some of my moments: here are Bo, the Duchess and Jerome; here is a skinny, teenaged Solomon Burke; here is the unregenerate spirit of rock & roll in the person of Jerry Lee; here are moments to remember—or invent.

I'll never forget the first time I met Michael Ochs, on the telephone. I was putting together pictures for the book I was then working on, *Lost Highway*, and Michael said he had some dynamite shots of Bobby "Blue" Bland—but there was one I couldn't have. It was a live shot of Bobby playing a Houston club in the '50s, and Michael was saving it for a book of his own. By the end of the conversation Michael had persuaded himself—without any prompting from me—that I should have the photograph, that it *belonged* in my book, that he'd get a chance to use it himself some day anyway. Well, here it is now, as eloquent in this context as it could possibly be, with Bobby surrounded by such legendary Duke Records stablemates as Little Junior Parker, Johnny Ace and Clarence "Gatemouth" Brown, the fans still clutching, the spotlight still shining, the process still impeccably in place.

ROCK ARCHIVES is a collection of just such unlikely juxtapositions—classic shots and rarities, household names and obscurities, performers who present themselves with touching innocence or, alternately, in poses calculated to win our admiration and affection. What is revealed in the end is never altogether predictable. Candor is not always candid; the pose often says more, and sometimes less, than the poseur intends. There are glimpses of mortality in youth and indomitable cries of affirmation simply in survival. Perhaps we should simply take this volume, then, as an unanticipated bonanza, a feast so rich and varied that it cannot be savored all at once but should be sampled one course at a time, with different courses appealing to different palates and suiting various moods at various times.

That, after all, is the true collector's attitude; at least it is the omnivorous collector's attitude. "When you're a collector," says Michael, "it gets to the point where it's going to drive you crazy if you try to keep up with everything. So you specialize in reggae or doo-wop or whatever. That's the only way you can come close to a complete collection. I prefer the crazy way!" Michael's real satisfaction, though, comes not from accumulating but from disseminating. I think the greatest pleasure he gets is imagining the gasp of surprise, the pleasure of recognition that readers/viewers/listeners are likely to get on each of his projects. I know. I looked at many of these pictures almost under Michael's direct scrutiny. "Oh wow!" I would exclaim as I came across some unlikely appearance by a member of my personal pantheon, some shot of Elvis in Tupelo at the Mississippi-Alabama Fair, an unrecognizable George Clinton presiding over a not-so-funkadelic parliament, or Ersel Hickey (again!) with a young and slender Johnny Cash. Every expression of astonishment on my part, every intake of breath would bring Michael running, to expound upon the background, circumstances and provenance of each picture, with an enthusiasm at least equal to my own. That is the kind of treat that lies in store for each reader—not Michael's exegeses but the pictures themselves, the thrill of discovery and the exclamation of delight that is the payoff for all of us in the end.

Part I MITOSIS

Late '40s to Late '50s

1

2

◄ *Singing the Blues*

Among the earliest blues artists to
have an impact on rock & roll was
T-Bone Walker (2), the first guitarist
to have a rhythm-guitar player and
so be free to play lead only. Walker
wrote and recorded the standard
"Stormy Monday," and as shown
here (1), preceded Jimi Hendrix in
guitar showmanship by over two
decades. Arthur "Big Boy" Crudup
(5) recorded many sides between
1940 and 1954, including the
original version of his "That's All
Right," Elvis Presley's 1954
commercial debut. Roy Brown (3)
wrote "Good Rockin' Tonight" in
1947 and recorded it the next year.
His gospel-style vocals have
influenced singers from Jackie
Wilson to B. B. King. Wynonie Harris
(4) also recorded "Good Rockin'
Tonight," which is considered by
many to have been the first rock &
roll song.

3

4

5

1

2

3

5

4

6

✑ *Singing the Blues*

Jimmy Reed (1; 4, right) was one of the first blues musicians to move successfully into pop. His lazy vocals and fervent harp playing were widely emulated. His best-known songs are "You Don't Have to Go" (1955), "Honest I Do" (1957) and "Big Boss Man" (1961). Guitarist John Lee Hooker (2) also exposed the blues to a wider audience. In 1949, he recorded "Boogie Chillen," and later hit with "I'm in the Mood" and "Boom Boom." Texas guitarist/singer Lightnin' Hopkins (5) recorded from the '40s through the '70s. His inventive style has been copied, but his songs, though extremely influential, were generally too personal to be sustained in cover versions. In 1948, pianist Amos Milburn's (3) "Chicken Shack Boogie" sold 1 million copies. He later recorded "One Scotch, One Bourbon, One Beer" and "Bad Bad Whiskey." Johnny Moore's Three Blazers (6) had several R&B hits, including "Walking Blues" and "Driftin' Blues," with Charles Brown (6, bottom middle; 7). Brown's solo hits were "Black Night" and "Seven Long Days."

7

1

◊◊ *Singing the Blues*

Between 1951 and 1958, Muddy Waters (2) (born McKinley Morganfield) had a dozen chart singles. The King of the Blues, Waters (here with Chess Records president Marshall Chess) recorded "Rollin' Stone," "I'm Your Hoochie Coochie Man," "Got My Mojo Workin'" and "Mannish Boy." Waters influenced and later performed with the Rolling Stones and Johnny Winter. Singer Howlin' Wolf (1) (Chester Burnett) was discovered by Ike Turner in 1948. His songs—"Smokestack Lightnin'," "Spoonful," "Little Red Rooster" and others—were frequently covered by rock groups in the late '60s. In 1947, Little Walter (3) (Marion Walter Jacobs), the major innovator in jazz-blues harmonica, arrived in Chicago, where he later played with Muddy and almost every other Chess Records artist. Guitar Slim (4) (Eddie Jones) recorded 1954's biggest blues hit, "The Things That I Used to Do," with Ray Charles on piano. Blues accordionist Clifton Chenier (5) is the king of Zydeco music and still maintains a wide following.

3

2

4

5

♪~ *Singing the Blues*

Singer/guitarist B. B. King is the foremost modern bluesman. King (7, with Johnny Otis) was born in Mississippi, but moved to Memphis, where he was nicknamed the Beale Street Blues Boy, shortened to B. B. He's cut hundreds of sides since his 1951 hit, "Three O'Clock Blues," including two million-sellers, "Every Day I Have the Blues" (1955) and "The Thrill Is Gone" (1969). Roy Milton, here with the Solid Senders (5) and his fan club (6), was a drummer/singer from Los Angeles, who monopolized the R&B chart from 1946 to 1952. Freddie King (1) began recording in 1956. His best-known hit was "Hideaway." Albert King's (2) songs included "Bad Luck Blues" (1953) and "Born under a Bad Sign" (1967). Lowell Fulson (4) was responsible for "Every Day I Have the Blues" (1950) and "Tramp" (1967). Pee Wee Crayton (3) was a major blues guitarist, whose biggest hit was 1949's "I Love You So."

5

6

7

5

✒ *Crooners and Criers*

From the late '40s to the late '50s, Sarah Vaughan's (4) sassy but silky singing graced dozens of hits, including 1959's "Broken Hearted Melody." One of the best jazz and pop vocalists ever, Ella Fitzgerald (2) wrote and recorded "A Tisket a Tasket." Dinah Washington (3), the Queen of the Harlem Blues, was the lead singer with Lionel Hampton's band from 1942 to 1946. Her biggest pop hit was "What a Diff'rence a Day Makes" (1959). The Treniers (5) were a gymnastic show band that at one time or another included from one to four of the Trenier brothers. They recorded "Say Hey" with Willie Mays in 1954. The Delta Rhythm Boys (6), a gospel harmony group, were known for such songs as "Dry Bones." The Mills Brothers (1) have been a major recording and touring act for over three decades. Their most famous songs include "Paper Doll" (1943), "Someday" (1949) and "Glow Worm" (1952).

6

1

~~ *Crooners and Criers*

Five years after Peggy Lee (3) began
singing with Benny Goodman, she
went Top Ten with Little Willie
John's "Fever" (1953); her last big
hit was 1969's "Is That All There Is."
During Doris Day's (1) three years
with the Les Brown Orchestra, she
hit Number One with "Sentimental
Journey" (1945) and continued to
top the chart with "Whatever Will
Be, Will Be (Que Sera, Sera)" (1956).
One of the first major '50s crooners,
Frankie Laine (6) had two Number
One hits: "That Lucky Old Sun" and
"Mule Train" (1949). Eddie Fisher
(2), whose 1953 Number One was
"Oh, My Papa," married actress
Debbie Reynolds in 1955. He left her
three years later for Elizabeth
Taylor; his career never recovered.
Tony Bennett (4) is best known for
1962's "I Left My Heart in San
Francisco." Johnnie Ray (5) was one
of the first male singers to drop the
cool stance; in fact, he would
actually cry onstage. His big hit was
1951's "Cry."

2

4

5

3

6

13

♫ *Crooners and Criers*

The Ames Brothers (3, with Marilyn
Monroe) first hit with the Number
One "Rag Mop" in 1951. They had
later hits, but Ed (second from right)
went on to greater fame as Daniel
Boone's TV Indian sidekick Mingo.
The Four Aces' (2) best-known hit
was the movie title theme "Love
Is a Many-Splendored Thing"
(1955). The Crew-Cuts (1) had their
top singles from covers of R&B
tunes: "Sh-Boom" (1954), "Earth
Angel" and "Koko Mo" (1955). Like
the Crew-Cuts, the Four Lads (4)
hailed from Canada. They sang
background on Johnnie Ray's "Cry,"
and had their own hits with
"Moments to Remember" (1955),
"No Not Much," "Standing on the
Corner" (1956), "Who Needs You"
and "Put a Light in the Window"
(1957). The Four Freshmen (5) were
just that when they first got together
in the early '50s. Their smooth
harmonies, like those in their 1956
hit "Graduation Day," influenced the
Beach Boys, among others.

1

2

14

1

2

3

4

❦ *Crooners and Criers*

Della Reese (3) began as a gospel singer with Mahalia Jackson. She went pop with "And That Reminds Me" (1957) and "Don't You Know" (1959). Despite her enormous following, Nina Simone (4) had only one major pop hit, 1959's "I Loves You, Porgy." Eartha Kitt (6) hit the Top Ten twice, with "C'est Si Bon" (1953) and "Santa Baby." Ex-heavyweight boxer Roy Hamilton (5) was one of the biggest black stars of the early '50s. His hits included "Ebb Tide" (1954) and "Unchained Melody" (1955). The McGuire Sisters (2) had several hits with such covers as "Sincerely" (1955). Les Paul and Mary Ford's (1) two Number One singles were "How High the Moon" (1951) and "Vaya con Dios" (1953). Paul pioneered the electric guitar, multitrack recording and the Gibson model guitar that bears his name.

5

6

1

2

3

18

✒ *Crooners and Criers*

Two years after her chart debut,
Patti Page's (4) "The Tennessee
Waltz" (1950) went to Number One,
followed by "How Much Is That
Doggie in the Window" (1953),
"Cross Over the Bridge" (1954) and
"Hush, Hush, Sweet Charlotte"
(1965). Kay Starr's (1) biggest hits
were "Bonaparte's Retreat" (1950)
and the Number One "Wheel of
Fortune" (1952). Dinah Shore's (5)
pop hits ran from 1941 to 1957; her
"Buttons and Bows" was Number
One in 1948. Joni James's (3) hits
included "Why Don't You Believe
Me" (1952) and "Little Things Mean
a Lot" (1960). At age eighteen,
Teresa Brewer (2), a former child
actress, recorded "Music, Music,
Music," a 1950 Number One.

5

6

7

🎵 *T for Tennessee*

The Singing Cowboy, Gene Autry (1), made Western movies and great records. "The Last Roundup" (1934) and "Tumbling Tumbleweed" (1935). Hank Williams (5) was the father of modern country music. He died at age twenty-nine on New Year's Day, 1953. But his music—the classic "I'm So Lonesome I Could Cry," "Jambalaya," "Hey, Good Lookin'" and "Your Cheatin' Heart" —are still recorded today. Hank Snow (7), the Singing Ranger, was managed by Col. Parker, who booked the young Elvis Presley on his tours. Snow's songs included "The Golden Rocket" and "Moving On" (1950). Jim Reeves's (8) biggest hits were "Four Walls" (1957) and "He'll Have to Go" (1960). Eddy Arnold's (6) best-known tune was "Bouquet of Roses." Kitty Wells (3) was the Queen of Country Music, with "Poison in Your Heart" and "Making Believe." Patsy Cline's (4) recording debut was 1957's "Walking after Midnight." She died in a plane crash six years later. Slim Whitman's (2) "Rosemarie" was a Number One pop hit in England for ten weeks in 1955.

8

~ *T for Tennessee*

Among Webb Pierce's (4) biggest hits was the classic drinking song "There Stands the Glass" (1953). His later hits included "In the Jailhouse Now" (1955) and "I Ain't Never" (1959). One of Pierce's protégés was Faron Young (1), who later became one of the most popular country crossover artists of the mid-'50s. Among his best-known records are "Live Fast, Love Hard, Die Young," "It's a Great Life If You Don't Weaken (But Who Wants to Be Strong)" (1955) and "Hello Walls" (1961). From Waco, Texas, Hank Thompson (3) brought Western Swing back to pop with "Wild Side of Life," and continued working in the genre through the '60s. Kitty Wells's "It Wasn't God Who Made Honky-Tonk Angels" was an answer to "Wild Side." Legendary guitarist Merle Travis (2) played on countless country & western records. He also had hits with "Divorce Me C.O.D.," "So Round, So Firm, So Fully Packed," "No Vacancy" and "Cincinnati Lou." He wrote Tennessee Ernie Ford's 1955 Number One hit "Sixteen Tons." Travis invented the now-standard three-finger picking style.

4

◆ *T for Tennessee*

Don Gibson (2) was the biggest writer of pop country hits in the '50s and '60s. His tunes include "Oh Lonesome Me," "I Can't Stop Loving You" (1960) and the 1973 Number One country hit "Woman (Sensuous Woman)." Stonewall Jackson's (5) biggest pop hit was 1959's "Waterloo." Ferlin Husky's (4) "Gone" (1957) was followed by "Wings of a Dove." Sonny James (3) started his two decades of hits with "Young Love" in 1956, backed by his group, the Southern Gentlemen. Marty Robbins (1) was one of the best pop singers in country. His hits included "Singing the Blues" (1956), "A White Sport Coat," "The Story of My Life" (1957), "El Paso" (1960) and "Devil Woman" (1962). He died of a heart ailment in 1983. Behind each of these country stars was producer/ guitarist Chet Atkins (6). During his early career, Atkins played behind Mother Maybelle and the Carter Family at the Grand Ole Opry. In the late '50s, he became the head of A&R for RCA in Nashville. There he produced many artists, including Elvis Presley, Hank Snow and Jim Reeves. His own singles included "Teensville" and "Bo Bo Stick Beat" from the '50s.

1

2

3

4

5

6

1

2

3

4

5

~♪ *T for Tennessee*

Though Homer and Jethro (3) were known as country satirists, Jethro Burns was considered one of country's finest musicians. Among their hits was "That Hound Dog in the Window." Bluegrass greats the Wilburn Brothers (5) were well known throughout country and pop. Their hits included "Go Away with Me" (1956) and "Which One Is to Blame" (1959). They toured nationally and later founded their own management company whose roster included Loretta Lynn. Marvin Rainwater (2) scored in 1957 with "Gonna Find Me a Bluebird." That same year Bobby Helms (1) hit with "Fraulein," "My Special Angel" and "Jingle Bell Rock." The Browns (6)—Jim Ed, Maxine and Bonnie— had hits with "The Three Bells" (1959) and "The Old Lamplighter" (1960). One of Jerry Lee Lewis's cousins, Mickey Gilley (4), recorded "Room Full of Roses" in 1974, nearly twenty years after his recording debut. He founded Gilley's Club in Texas.

6

1

〜 *Crazy, Man, Crazy*

Compared to contemporaries like
Little Richard, Bill Haley (5, 6) was a
most unlikely rock star. He was
overweight, over thirty and not
overly impressive onstage. But in
1954, Haley recorded "Rock around
the Clock," the first Number One
rock & roll hit and the tune that,
when used in *Blackboard Jungle*,
linked rock music and juvenile
delinquency. It hit in 1955 and
eventually sold 25 million copies.
Haley founded a country & western
group in 1949; by 1952, he had
changed their name to Bill Haley and
His Comets (1, 4) and in 1954
recorded Big Joe Turner's "Shake,
Rattle and Roll." The Comets were
the first internationally famous rock
group; their appearances sparked
riots in Europe. Haley died in 1981 at
fifty-five, a broken man. The Comets'
success inspired imitators: Freddy
Bell and the Bellboys (2). The
Jodimars (3) were formed in 1956 by
the original Comets.

2

3

4

5

6

5

4

∿ *Big Boss Men*

With the exception of Al Hibbler, none of these R&B stars had widespread pop success, yet their work helped shape rock & roll. Joe Turner (4), the Boss of the Blues, had been an R&B star since the early '30s. Though Turner had only two pop singles—"Corrina Corrina" (1956) and "Honey Hush" (1953)—his R&B hits were often covered successfully by white artists. A sanitized version of his sexy "Shake, Rattle and Roll" was a hit for Bill Haley. In contrast, Al Hibbler (1), a blind singer whose first R&B hit came in 1948, had three Top Ten hits: "Unchained Melody," "He" and "After the Lights Go Down Low"

(1955-56). In 1949, Stick McGhee (3), Brownie McGhee's brother, recorded "Drinkin' Wine Spo-dee-o-dee," since covered in over 100 versions; one of the best known was by Jerry Lee Lewis. Percy Mayfield (2) hit big on the R&B charts in 1950 with "Please Send Me Someone to Love." Ivory Joe Hunter's (5) "I Almost Lost My Mind," a million-seller in 1950, became a Number One hit for Pat Boone in 1956, the same year Hunter made his pop-chart debut with "Since I Met You Baby."

✒ *T for Texas*

Don Robey (6, with Johnny Otis)
founded Peacock Records in 1949.
His first release was Clarence
"Gatemouth" Brown's (5) "Mary Is
Fine." Three years later Robey took
over Duke and there released Willie
Mae (Big Mama) Thornton's (1, 3)
"Hound Dog" (1953). Thornton
wrote "Ball and Chain." One of
Robey's most celebrated signings
was Bobby "Blue" Bland (7, 8), a
contemporary bluesman whose hits
included "Farther Up the Road"
(1957) and "Turn On Your Love
Light" (1961). Johnny Ace (4), who
had begun as Bland's pianist, was on
his way to establishing a recording
career when he shot himself to
death in a backstage game of
Russian roulette on Christmas Eve,
1954. Ace's posthumous hit was
1955's "Pledging My Love." Little
Junior Parker (2), who wrote
"Mystery Train," recorded "Sweet
Home Chicago" (1958).

1

3

2

4

2

1

 ***Crazy Little Mamas***

Ruth Brown, Faye Adams and
LaVern Baker were the leading
female R&B vocalists of the '50s.
From 1949 to the late '50s, Ruth
Brown (1), a.k.a. Miss Rhythm, was
Atlantic's biggest-selling artist with
such hits as "Teardrops from My

Eyes," "Mama (He Treats Your
Daughter Mean)," "Five-Ten-
Fifteen Hours" and "Lucky Lips"
(1950-57). Faye "Atomic" Adams's
(2) first hit was 1953's "Shake a
Hand," a song about racial
understanding that has since
become a standard. Her other hits
were "I'll Be True" and "Hurts Me to
My Heart" (1953-54). LaVern Baker
(3) began her career billed as Little
Miss Sharecropper. Her best-known
hits include "Tweedlee Dee," "Jim
Dandy" and "I Cried a Tear"
(1955-59). Baker was also one of the
few artists to speak out publicly
against white acts blatantly copying
R&B records, a trend that denied
many black artists the fame they
deserved.

3

〜 *Swingin' like a Rusty Ax*

Before the electric guitar emerged as the key lead instrument in rock, many great records featured the sax solo. One of the greatest honkers was "Bull Moose" Jackson (3), who sold millions of records in the late '40s, among them "Little Girl, Don't Cry" and "Why Don't You Haul Off and Love Me." Big Jay McNeely (4) played frantically, often contorting his body and blowing on his back. His bands wore shirts that glowed in the dark. McNeely wrote "There Is Something on Your Mind." Joe Houston (5) recorded "All Night Long." Sil Austin's (7) 1956 pop hit was "Slow Walk." A noted jazz musician, Illinois Jacquet (2) had an R&B hit in 1952 with "Port of Rico." Sam "The Man" Taylor (8) led Alan Freed's band in the '50s. Also pictured here are studio honkers Choker Campbell (6) and Buddy Lucas (1).

4

5

6

7

8

⌁ *Birth of the Boogie*

Disc jockey Alan Freed (1) not only
coined and tried to copyright the
term rock & roll, but was the first to
bring the music and its artists to the
attention of the American public. In
1951, Freed joined Cleveland's WJW,
where for the next two years he
hosted the "Moondog Rock & Roll
Party" (4, 5). Freed's playlist
consisted primarily of R&B, but he
chose to call it rock & roll to sidestep
the stigma attached to black or
"race" records. In March 1952, he
staged the first large-scale rock
show, "The Moondog Coronation
Ball," at the Cleveland Arena. When
25,000 fans showed up to claim
10,000 seats, the show was canceled.
Freed constantly defended rock
music. "Anyone who says rock & roll
is a passing fad or a flash in the pan
has rocks in his head, dad," Freed
said. Here, a young Freed (6), and
with his family (2, 3, 7).

5

6

7

3

〜 *Birth of the Boogie*

By September 1954, when Freed
moved to WINS in New York City, he
seemed to have been vindicated (1,
with Dean Barlow). He staged
countless all-star bills at the
Brooklyn and New York Paramount
theaters (2) and other venues, was
the first major DJ to refuse to play
white covers of R&B songs and, in
1956 alone, starred in three rock
movies (*Rock around the Clock,
Rock, Rock, Rock* and *Don't Knock
the Rock*). But the controversy rock
had aroused caught up to him. In
1958, he was arrested for inciting a
riot at a show in Boston. Though
soon acquitted, Freed was quickly
blacklisted as a result of the
government's payola investigations.
Payola was an illegal but widely
accepted industry practice.
Certainly, dozens were guilty, but
lacking support and any trace of
respectability or remorse, Freed
took the fall, pleading guilty and
receiving a suspended sentence in
1962. He died on January 20, 1965, of
uremia at age forty-two.

4

5

6

7

♪ *Tell Tchaikovsky the News*

Chuck Berry was rock & roll's first black sex symbol to cross over to pop, and its single most influential artist after Elvis Presley. Although Berry didn't begin recording until he was twenty-nine, his songs, which freely mixed country, blues and rock, gave to white teens an exuberant vision of rebellious, yet confident, fun and sexuality. Berry's "Maybellene," "Roll Over, Beethoven," "School Day," "Rock & Roll Music," "Sweet Little Sixteen," "Johnny B. Goode," "Carol" and "Reelin' & Rockin'" were biographical, yet told the story of a generation. Berry was born in St. Louis, and, during his teens, served time in a reform school for attempted robbery. Upon his release, he earned a degree in cosmetology. He later performed with Muddy Waters, who got him

signed to Chess, where in 1955 he recorded "Maybellene." From then until 1962, when he began serving a two-year sentence for bringing a minor over the state line for immoral purposes, Berry had nine Top Forty hits. In 1972, he scored his sole Number One, the childish yet risqué "My Ding-A-Ling."

~ *Bo Diddley, Bo Diddley*

In the '50s, the major innovator of rock & roll guitar and stage moves, Bo Diddley, perfected the chunky, hambone rhythm that bears his name. It's since been the heart of songs by dozens of artists, from the early Stones to the Pretenders. Diddley also pioneered the use of controlled distortion and designed and built his own elaborately shaped, custom-built guitars. As a child, Ellas McDaniel moved to Chicago. There he played clubs until 1955, when he cut "Bo Diddley" for Chess's sister label Checker and played guitar on a couple of Chuck Berry tunes, including "Memphis." Although Diddley had but one pop Top Twenty hit, his influence ranged far and wide: Elvis Presley is said to have studied his stage moves, the Pretty Things were named after one of his songs, and the Animals ostensibly saluted him as "the rock & roll senior general" in "The Story of Bo Diddley." "Mona," "You Can't Judge a Book by Its Cover," "I'm a Man" and "Who Do You Love" are among the R&B songs most often covered by '60s British groups. Diddley toured and recorded with his group, which included maracas player Jerome Green (4, front) and Diddley's half-sister, the Duchess (5).

1

2

♪ *I Was the One*

While Elvis Presley wasn't the first rock & roller, he was the most important, inspiring generations the world over. He is the King. Presley (1) was nineteen when Sam Phillips released his "That's All Right" in July 1954. Recorded at Sun with guitarist Scotty Moore (2, left; 4) and bassist Bill Black (2, right), the song became a local hit, and less than two years later, Presley's manager, Col. Tom Parker (3, left), orchestrated Presley's move to RCA. From 1956 through 1977, Presley charted over 100 Top Forty hits, including "Hound Dog," "Heartbreak Hotel," "Love Me Tender," "Don't Be Cruel" and "Let Me Be Your Teddy Bear," some with vocal backing by the Jordanaires (5). During the mid-to-late '50s, Presley was the object of an extraordinary fan hysteria and the subject of much controversy. He was a poor, white Southern boy who sang Negro music, while shaking his hips and driving everyone wild.

3

4

5

48

4

5

⌇ *I Was the One*

After a late-'50s stint in the army and twenty-nine nondescript movies, Presley made his comeback in late 1968 in an hour-long television special. The success of *Elvis* heralded the start of his Vegas-coliseum tours. Grueling but lucrative, this phase of his career earned him millions of new fans and untold wealth. More than any single achievement, it is Presley's legend that endures. In every way, he embodied a dark yet alluring facet of the American dream. His voice was simply the most magnificent ever recorded. His extraordinary looks and cocky, warm sexuality were both a threat and pleasure. Yet Elvis remained the perpetual outsider, his fame overshadowing every day of his natural life. Elvis died on August 16, 1977. Here, Elvis with Johnny Cash (4), Nudie the Tailor (5), Sal Mineo (6), Brenda Lee (3), at "The Louisiana Hayride" (2) and after a 1956 Oakland concert (1).

6

❧ *Put Your Cat Clothes On*

Johnny Cash's recordings have
encompassed country, rockabilly,
folk, gospel, protest and novelties.
Cash (1) started at Sun, where he cut
"Cry, Cry, Cry" (1955), "Folsom
Prison Blues" and "I Walk the Line"
(1956). Successful though they were,
his early hits were eclipsed by the
hugely popular *Live at Folsom
Prison* (1968) and 1969's Top Five
novelty, "A Boy Named Sue." Johnny
Horton (2, right, with Cash; 4,
middle) was a pop success with
"The Battle of New Orleans" (1959),
"North to Alaska" and "Sink the
Bismarck" (1960). In 1954, he
married Hank Williams's widow,
Billie Jean. In November 1960, on
the way home from playing Austin's
Skyline, Horton was killed in a car
crash. Ironically, the Skyline had
been the scene of Williams's last
date as well. Also pictured: Billie
Jean Horton and Al Jones (3);
Johnny Cash with Ersel Hickey (5).

〜 *Put Your Cat Clothes On*

Rockabilly is a wild-spirited
distillation of country and R&B
and its home was the Sun label
in Memphis. Carl Perkins (1, 2, 3)
wrote and recorded "Blue Suede
Shoes," the first song to top the pop,
country and R&B charts. At his peak,
Perkins was laid up for nine months
after a 1956 car crash that killed his
brother Jay; he never regained his
momentum. His "Honey Don't" and
"Everybody's Tryin' to Be My Baby"
were covered by the Beatles. Jerry
Lee Lewis's cousin Carl McVoy (5)
cut a dozen songs for Sun affiliate
Phillips International, but only "You
Are My Sunshine" was released.
McVoy later joined Bill Black's
Combo. Charlie Feathers (6,
middle), the genre's most celebrated
cult figure, wrote Elvis's "I Forgot to
Remember to Forget." Cliff, Ed and
Barbara Thomas (4) backed other
Sun artists and released a few
unsuccessful singles.

2

3

4

5

6

1

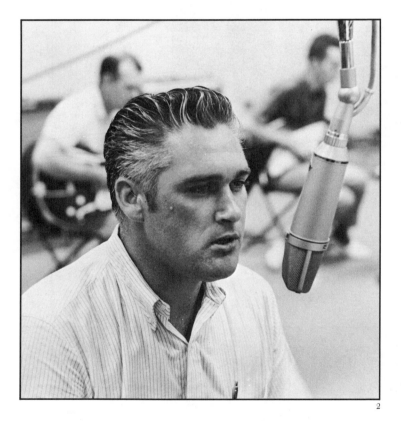

2

3

4

5

6

〜 *Put Your Cat Clothes On*

Charlie Rich (2) recorded "Lonely Weekends" for Phillips in 1960 and "Mohair Sam" for Smash in 1965. But he didn't have a Number One hit until he went country with 1973's "The Most Beautiful Girl." Billy Lee Riley (6) formed the Little Green Men—whose stage costumes were made from green pool-table felt—after his "Red Hot" and "Flyin' Saucers Rock 'n' Roll," both covered in the '70s by Robert Gordon, became hits. Carl Mann (1) recorded "Mona Lisa" in 1959, but Sam Phillips refused to release it until after Conway Twitty's version of it charted. Sonny Burgess and the Pacers (5, Sonny second from left), who often toured with Twitty, had "My Bucket's Got a Hole in It" and "Red Headed Woman." Edwin Bruce (3), who recorded for Sun as a teen, wrote Waylon and Willie's "Mammas, Don't Let Your Babies Grow Up to Be Cowboys." Detroit's Johnny Powers (4) recorded four sides for Sun in 1959.

5

~~ *Put Your Cat Clothes On*

In the wake of Elvis's initial success, an audience developed for other rockabilly singers. Bob Luman (3) cut "Red Hot" (1957) and "Let's Think about Living" (1960). Billy "Crash" Craddock's (1) "I'm Tore Up" bombed in the United States, but did well in Australia. He worked in construction until his 1971 comeback with "Knock Three Times." Bobby Lee Trammell (5) wanted Memphis disc jockeys to play his "You Mostest Girl" so badly that he regularly scaled radio station transmitter towers and refused to come down until the jocks complied. The Collins Kids (2)—Larry and Lorrie—recorded "Rock Boppin' Baby." Larry later cowrote Tanya Tucker's "Delta Dawn." Roy Orbison, here with the Teen Kings (6), had his first hit with "Ooby Dooby" for Sun, before he went on to greater success. Cincinnati's Dale Wright (4, center, with the Wright Guys) had a pair of minor hits in 1958—"She's Neat" and "Please Don't Do It."

6

1

2

3

⌁ *Put Your Cat Clothes On*

There were several female rockabillies, but Wanda Jackson (2, with Her Party Timers) was the wildest. Her label, Capitol, saw her as the female Gene Vincent, and, in fact, the Blue Caps played on several of her records. Her biggest hits were "Let's Have a Party" (1960) and "Right or Wrong" (1961). Ersel Hickey (3) hailed from Buffalo, but his style was rockabilly. In 1958, he charted his only hit, "Bluebirds over the Mountain." Hickey also wrote "Don't Let the Rain Come Down" for the Serendipity Singers. Ronnie Self (1) began recording in 1957 at eighteen years of age. His singles included "Bob-A-Lena," and he wrote Brenda Lee's "Sweet Nothin's" and "I'm Sorry." Justin Tubb (5), country star Ernest Tubb's son, recorded "Rock It on Down to My House" (1953). And Johnny Carroll (4) recorded the title song for and was the star of the only '50s rockabilly movie, *Rock, Baby, Rock It*.

4

5

1

2

3

♪ *Put Your Cat Clothes On*

Narvel Felts (5) had to pick cotton in order to afford his first guitar. He hit the charts in 1960 with "Honey Love." Thirteen years later, he came back with the country smash "Drift Away." Joe Bennett and the Sparkletones (6), none of whom was over seventeen, recorded the popular "Black Slacks" in 1957. The group broke up the following year, after it was clear that being under age meant few legal bookings. Janis Martin (4), billed as the female Elvis, was only fifteen when she cut "Will You, Willyum" in 1956. Sanford Clark (2) hit the Top Ten in 1956 with Phoenix disc jockey Lee Hazlewood's "The Fool." Warner Mack (1), recorded "Is It Wrong (for Loving You)" (1957) and "Roc-A-Chicka" (1958). Also pictured: singer/songwriter Mack Vickery (3).

4

5

6

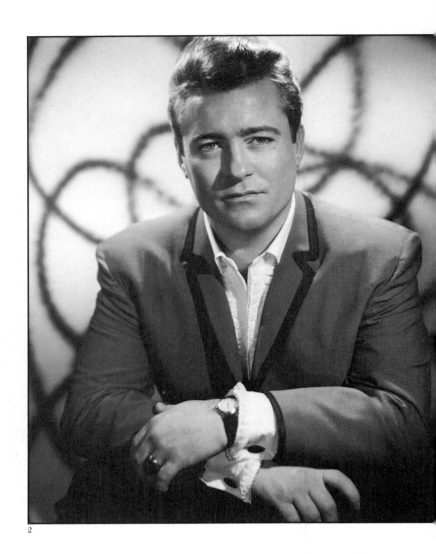

⁓ *Put Your Cat Clothes On*

The Burnettes—brothers Johnny and Dorsey, and later sons Rocky and Billy—are rockabilly's first family. While Dorsey (2) worked with Elvis Presley at Crown Electric in the early '50s, Johnny (3, 4) and Johnny Cash were selling dishes door to door, usually on opposite sides of the same street. In the mid-'50s, Johnny, Dorsey and guitarist Paul Burlison formed the Rock 'n' Roll Trio (1), and soon won on *Ted Mack's Amateur Hour* three times in a row. This led to a recording contract and their classic "Train Kept A-Rollin'." The Trio disbanded in 1957, when the Burnette brothers moved to Los Angeles, where they became successful songwriters. In 1960, both had hits; Johnny's were "Dreamin'" and "You're Sixteen" and Dorsey's were "Tall Oak Tree" and "Hey Little One." Johnny was preparing a comeback when he drowned in 1964. His son, Rocky, had a 1980 hit, "Tired of Toein' the Line." Dorsey continued touring until his death in 1979, and his son, Billy, is also a recording artist.

4

∾ *Street Corner Symphonies*

Doo-wop, originally a multipart a cappella style, added lively rhythms and nonsense-syllable backgrounds to gospel harmonizing to create one of the best-loved rock genres. Between 1951 and 1959, the Clovers (5) had thirteen consecutive R&B hits before their 1956 pop debut, "Love, Love, Love." Their "Love Potion No. 9" (1959) was covered by dozens of artists, most notably the Searchers. The Orioles (1) began performing together in 1947. Between 1949 and 1953, they were one of the Apollo Theatre's biggest draws, with lead singer Sonny Til driving women wild with his ethereal voice and sensual moves. Their best-known hit was "Crying in the Chapel" (1953). The "5" Royales (3) included lead singer Lowman Pauling, the first guitarist to play his instrument at crotch level. Their 1961 "Dedicated to the One I Love" was a hit for the Shirelles the same year. The Chords' (2) "Sh-Boom" was one of the first R&B hits to gain massive pop acceptance. The Crests (4), with lead singer Johnny Maestro, had many hits, including 1958's "Sixteen Candles."

5

❧ *Street Corner Symphonies*

Jerry Wexler once called Clyde McPhatter (6) "the great, unique soul singer of all time." A gospel singer since fourteen, McPhatter joined Billy Ward's Dominoes (5, McPhatter at bottom) in 1950. Three years later McPhatter formed the Drifters, with whom he recorded "Money Honey," "Such a Night" and "Honey Love" before he was drafted in 1954; he is seen here on leave at the Apollo, with Ruth Brown and LaVern Baker (1). Upon his return, he launched his solo career with "Treasure of Love" (1956) and the million-selling "A Lover's Question" (1959). (Clyde's last major hit was "Lover Please" in 1962. He died in 1972 at thirty-eight.) Meanwhile, the Drifters (2) had several lead vocalists before disbanding in 1958. Their manager then bestowed the Drifters name on the Five Crowns, fronted by Ben E. King (3). This lineup had several more hits, including "There Goes My Baby," "This Magic Moment" and "Save the Last Dance for Me," King's last record with the group. With Rudy Lewis, the Drifters (4) recorded "On Broadway" and "Up on the Roof"; after Lewis died in 1964, Johnny Moore, an early McPhatter replacement, returned and appeared on "Under the Boardwalk."

6

1

✺ *Street Corner Symphonies*

Most doo-wop groups came and went within a year. The Turbans (6) ("When You Dance," 1955), the Nutmegs (5) ("Story Untold," 1955) and the Tune Weavers (4) ("Happy, Happy Birthday, Baby," 1957) are classic examples. The Dubs (1) had two hits in 1957, "Don't Ask Me (to Be Lonely)" and "Could This Be Magic." The Dell-Vikings (3), one of the first biracial rock groups, formed in Pittsburgh, where all of the members were serving in the air force. Two years later, they hit with "Come Go with Me" (recently revived by the Beach Boys), "Whispering Bells" and "Cool Shake." One member, Chuck Jackson, later pursued a solo career. Maurice Williams's "Little Darlin'" was the Gladiolas' (2) 1957 hit, which went Top Ten when covered by the Diamonds the same year.

2

3

Sincerely
THE TUNE WEAVERS

4

6

5

4

5

♪ *Street Corner Symphonies*

Frankie Lymon (1, 2, 3) was not only the youngest teen rock star, but one of the best young, male soprano lead singers ever. He formed the Teenagers with Sherman Garnes, Joe Negroni, Herman Santiago and Jimmy Merchant (5) in 1954. Two years later, when Lymon was just thirteen, the group hit with "Why Do Fools Fall in Love." In 1956, they followed with "I Want You to Be My Girl," "I Promise to Remember" and "The ABC's of Love." By the time Lymon went solo in 1957 and scored his only hit, "Goody Goody," he had developed a heroin habit. Both Lymon and the Teenagers attempted separate careers with minimal success. Lymon's addiction worsened and eventually killed him in 1968. But despite the brevity of his career, Lymon's impact was enormous. The Teen Chords (4) made his brother Lewis their lead singer on the basis of Frankie's success.

1

2

✍ *Street Corner Symphonies*

The Spaniels (3) are notable for being the first artists signed to the legendary Chicago label, Vee-Jay Records. They recorded "Goodnite, Sweetheart, Goodnite" in 1954, which only made the pop chart with the McGuire Sisters' cover. Labelmates with hits included the El Dorados (1) ("At My Front Door," 1955) and the Magnificents (5) ("Up on the Mountain," 1956). Here, a poster announces a 1956 Vee-Jay Cavalcade of Stars tour (2). The Moonglows (4) made their pop debut in 1955 with "Sincerely," also covered by the McGuire Sisters. Harvey Fuqua left the group in 1959. He subsequently married one of Berry Gordy's sisters and joined the family business, producing the Spinners and others for Motown. The Dells (6) first recorded "Oh, What a Night" in 1956; it was a hit again in 1969. The year before, they had made a tremendous comeback with "There Is" and "Stay in My Corner." The group continued to record through the mid-'70s.

3

4

5

6

1

♪~ *Street Corner Symphonies*

The Flamingos (1) had several hits, including "I'll Be Home," "Lovers Never Say Goodbye" and "I Only Have Eyes for You" (1956-59). Lee Andrews and the Hearts (4) got together in high school, and within two years had three hits, "Long Lonely Nights," "Teardrops" and "Try the Impossible" (1957-58). Otis Williams and the Charms' (2) two biggest hits were more successful in white cover versions: the million-selling "Hearts of Stone" (1955) and "Ivory Tower" (1956). The Cadillacs (3) were one of the first show groups with routines between songs. Their biggest hit was 1955's "Speedo." In 1956, Fred Parris and the Five Satins (5) recorded his "In the Still of the Nite," perhaps the most popular doo-wop ballad of all time, in the basement of a New Haven, Connecticut, church. Their followup hit was 1957's "To the Aisle."

2

74

3

4

5

1

2

✺ *Street Corner Symphonies*

The Ink Spots (3) were the first, most influential black vocal group. Formed in 1934, the group, which later included lead singer Bill Kenney, was the first to feature a tenor lead. Their earlier hits included the million-selling "If I Didn't Care" and "My Prayer." Their legacy grew through countless other vocal groups, the most successful of which was the Platters (1, 2), one of the first black groups to cross over to pop and the biggest-selling group in the '50s. Like the Ink Spots, the Platters also had a tenor lead, Tony Williams. Two of their hits, "My Prayer" and "To Each His Own," were remakes of Ink Spots recordings. From 1955 to 1960, the original Platters, featuring female singer Zola Taylor, had twelve Top Twenty hits, including "Only You (and You Alone)," "The Great Pretender," "(You've Got) the Magic Touch," "You'll Never Know," "Twilight Time," "Smoke Gets in Your Eyes" and "Harbor Lights."

3

~♪~ *Street Corner Symphonies*

Little Anthony (Gourdine) and the Imperials (1) made their chart debut in 1958 with "Tears on My Pillow," and continued to chart hits, including "Shimmy, Shimmy Ko-Ko-Bop," until they disbanded two years later. In 1964, they came back, and within six months, they released "I'm on the Outside (Looking In)," "Goin' Out of My Head" (1964) and "Hurt So Bad" (1965). The Silhouettes' (4) 1958 Number One was "Get a Job," still the quintessential doo-wop tune for its "Sha-na-na-na, sha-na-na-na-na" chorus. The Pastels' (5) 1958 hit was "Been So Long," featuring lead singer Big Dee Irwin (left)(Defosca Ervin). The Fiestas (6) recorded "So Fine" in 1959. The Sheppards (3) are best known for their "Island of Love," the Chargers (2) for their outrageous version of "Old McDonald."

3

4

5

6

1

2

3

❧ *A White Sport Coat*

The biggest '50s male clean teen was Pat Boone (5). A collegiate good guy, Boone debuted in 1955; the same year, he hit Number One with a cover of Fats Domino's "Ain't That a Shame." His later hits included "Love Letters in the Sand" and "April Love" (1957). Boone's younger brother, Nick Todd (7), had two minor 1957 hits, "Plaything" and "At the Hop." Andy Williams (3, with Boone) had sung with his older brothers before going solo with "Canadian Sunset," "Butterfly" and "Are You Sincere" (1956-58). Like Boone, Williams became a TV star. Jimmie Rodgers's (4, with wife) "Honeycomb," "Kisses Sweeter than Wine" and "Oh-Oh, I'm Falling in Love Again" (1957-58) were among the first attempts to homogenize folk and rockabilly into a pop style. Other shorter-lived stars include Charlie Gracie (6) ("Butterfly" and "Fabulous," 1957), Guy Mitchell (1), whose Number Ones were "Singing the Blues" (1956) and "Heartaches by the Number" (1959), and Rusty Draper (2), who is best known for 1957's "Freight Train."

5

6

7

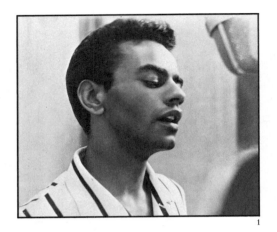

1

2

4

5

♪ *Wonderful, Wonderful*

Nat "King" Cole (2), born in the early '20s, fronted a jazz trio before beginning his solo career as a singer/pianist in the mid-'40s. His style—polished and sophisticated, yet warm—kept him on the charts from 1944's "Straighten Up and Fly Right" until his death in February 1966 of cancer. The Chordettes (4, 5), from Sheboygan, Wisconsin, were an important link between '50s pop and rock & roll. Five years after their 1949 debut on Arthur Godfrey's show, they hit Number One with "Mr. Sandman." Later hits included "Eddie My Love," "Born to Be with You" and "Lollipop" (1956-58). Between 1957, when he debuted with "Wonderful! Wonderful!," and the mid-'60s, Johnny Mathis (1, 3) was the king of the romantic ballad, "make-out music." In 1957 alone, he charted with "It's Not for Me to Say," "Chances Are," "The Twelfth of Never," "Wild Is the Wind" and "No Love (but Your Love)." His *Greatest Hits* (1958) was still on the chart over nine years later.

83

✎ *Say It Loud*

For over two decades, James Brown has been Soul Brother Number One, the Hardest Working Man in Show Business, and one of the most successful and innovative black entertainers in history. Born in 1928 in Tennessee, Brown danced in the streets of Augusta, Georgia, as a child. After a three-year stint in a juvenile detention home, he tried his hand at semipro sports before becoming a gospel singer. In the mid-'50s, he formed the Famous Flames (4), with whom he recorded his first R&B hit, "Please Please Please." Later, he hit the road with a crack backup band, the J.B.'s, and before long his shows were legendary. Doing splits, spins, knee-drops and one-legged shimmies, Brown would end the show with several reprises, during which a Flame would drape a cape over the fallen Brown, only to see him jump up and return to his woman, the microphone, then restage the act again (1). With "Papa's Got a Brand New Bag," "I Got You (I Feel Good)," "Cold Sweat (Part 1)," "I Got the Feelin'," "Say It Loud—I'm Black and I'm Proud," "Mother Popcorn" and "Hot Pants," Brown virtually wrote the book on funk.

1

2

3

4

5

4

↝ *Finger Poppin' Time*

Hank Ballard and the Midnighters, Little Willie John and Screamin' Jay Hawkins are each the foremost practitioners of three widely disparate, influential styles. Little Willie (5) was the most poignant blues singer in rock. In 1956, he recorded the original "Fever," which he cowrote. Twelve years later, he died of pneumonia in a Washington state prison, where he was serving time for manslaughter. Hank Ballard and the Midnighters (1) recorded the original "Every Beat of My Heart" in 1952 as the Royals. Two years later, they released the sexually explicit "Work with Me, Annie." Solo, Ballard (2) recorded the original version of his "The Twist," as well as "Finger Poppin' Time," "Let's Go, Let's Go, Let's Go" (1960), "The Hoochi Coochi Coo" and "The Switch-A-Roo" (1961). Screamin' Jay Hawkins (3, 4), rock's first theatrical eccentric, recorded "I Put a Spell on You" in 1956 while drunk. Known to take the stage in a coffin, Hawkins was the creator of shock rock.

5

✒ *Great Balls of Fire*

Jerry Lee Lewis is the devil's evangelist, an unrepentant singer/pianist/wild man. Lewis whipped longing and danger into an enticing, palpable tension. While Elvis seemed merely suggestive, Jerry Lee was instructional, with such lyrics as "all you gotta do, honey, is kinda stand in one spot, just wiggle it around a little bit . . ." on "Whole Lot of Shakin' Going On." But Jerry Lee's wild arrogance wasn't an act. He had charted three Top Ten hits on Sun—"Whole Lot of Shakin'," "Great Balls of Fire" (1957) and "Breathless" (1958)—and

seemed destined to equal Presley, until he admitted that his third wife was his fourteen-year-old third cousin. Public reaction was swift and unforgiving. After years of playing dives, he reemerged in the late '60s a rediscovered hero and launched an impressive country career. His Top Ten country hits include "Another Place, Another Time," "What's Made Milwaukee Famous (Has Made a Loser Out of Me)" (1968) and "She Even Woke Me Up to Say Goodbye" (1969). He still drives audiences wild with his leering delivery, pumpin' piano and untamed, ageless style. Here, with the original trio (2), Buddy Holly (5) and in *High School Confidential* (1).

1

4

2

3

5

♫ *Crying in the Rain*

As soon as they could stand, brothers Don and Phil Everly were performing together on their folks' (Ike and Margaret's) country radio show. Don was twenty, Phil eighteen, when they had their first pop hit, "Bye Bye Love," in 1957. Between then and 1962, they had fifteen Top Ten singles, including "All I Have to Do Is Dream,"

"Devoted to You," "(Til) I Kissed You" (with backing by the Crickets), "Let It Be Me," "When Will I Be Loved" and "Crying in the Rain," all of which featured the finest, most unabashedly romantic close harmonies in rock & roll and influenced the Beatles, Dave Edmunds and Nick Lowe, among others. But out of the limelight, the two had been rivals all their lives; Don and the fair-haired Phil regularly duked it out before hitting the stage. Their partnership seemed to have ended for good in 1973, until their 1983 onstage reunion at London's Royal Albert Hall. Here, with Jack Kelly (3), the president of Warner Bros. Records (4) and in 1970 with Neil Diamond (6).

5

6

⌁ *Walking to New Orleans*

(Antoine) Fats Domino was the most popular practitioner of the New Orleans sound. During the '50s, no one except Elvis Presley sold more records than Domino, a portly singer/pianist, whose relaxed yet rollicking style is the essence of New Orleans R&B. Born in 1929, Domino began playing honky-tonks when he was ten. In the mid-'40s, he was discovered by bandleader/producer Dave Bartholomew and in 1949 signed to Imperial Records, where he cut his first million-seller, "The Fat Man." From 1955 to 1960, he had twenty-three gold singles and ten Top Ten hits, including "Ain't That a Shame," "I'm in Love Again," "Blueberry Hill," "I'm Walkin'," "Whole Lotta Loving" and "Walking to New Orleans." In addition to his importance in American music, his records were a major influence on Jamaican ska and reggae musicians. In 1968, Domino charted with a cover of the Beatles' "Lady Madonna." Here, Domino at an Imperial Records party with Eddie Cochran (4, right) and at home with songwriter Jimmy Donley (1).

1

2

✒ *Walking to New Orleans*

The sound of New Orleans influenced not only rock & roll, but a whole generation of reggae musicians. In 1952, Lloyd Price (1, with his father) recorded "Lawdy Miss Clawdy," with Fats Domino on piano. After two years in the service, Price returned with "Just Because" (1957), "Stagger Lee" and "Personality" (1959). Though Smiley Lewis's (7) biggest hit was "I Hear You Knocking" (1955), his "One Night (of Sin)," cleaned up and retitled "One Night (of Love)," was a 1958 hit for Elvis Presley. Shirley (Goodman) and (Leonard) Lee (5), the Sweethearts of the Blues, had a million-seller, "Let the Good Times Roll," in 1956. Later that year they charted with "I Feel Good." In 1961, Chris Kenner (2) wrote and recorded his biggest hit, "I Like It like That," and hit again in 1963 with "Land of 1000 Dances." Drummer Earl Palmer (3) set the style for New Orleans and rock in general. Saxophonist Lee Allen (4), who played on hits by Fats Domino and Little Richard, had a hit, 1958's "Walking with Mr. Lee." He currently plays with the Blasters. Also pictured, the Spiders (6), whose 1954 hit was "I Didn't Want to Do It."

1

2

3

5

6

4

7

⌁ *Walking to New Orleans*

"I am the Bronze Liberace, the King of Rock & Roll. I gave the Beatles their first break . . ." Billing himself as the King and the Queen of Rock, Little Richard Penniman was easily the most outrageous rocker of the '50s. Richard, a Georgia native, left home at thirteen. He made his first recordings for RCA in 1951, but didn't have a hit until 1956: his cleaned-up version of the originally obscene "Tutti-Frutti." His other hits —such as "Long Tall Sally," "Rip It Up," "Ready Teddy," "Jenny, Jenny," "Keep A-Knockin'" and "Good Golly Miss Molly"—sold over 4 million copies. But less than two years later Richard claimed to have had a religious experience, during which God told him to leave show biz, and dedicated himself to the Lord. Richard returned in the early '60s, with the Beatles (2) and the Stones as his opening acts. His band then included unknown guitarist Jimmy (later Jimi) Hendrix. Here, with Bill Haley (4).

1

2

3

4

97

✺ *Walking to New Orleans*

By the time Mac Rebennack (2) made his performing debut as Dr. John the Night Tripper in 1968, he had been working as a session keyboardist/guitarist/producer for over a decade. In colorful robes and headdresses and backed by a Mardi Gras-style band and singers, Dr. John (3) became a rock attraction. In addition to recording under his own name, Rebennack had worked with Phil Spector, Joe Tex, Frankie Ford and others. New Orleans's premier songwriter/producer Allen Toussaint (6) began recording as Tousan in the late '50s. He has produced Ernie K-Doe, Lee Dorsey, Jessie Hill, Chris Kenner, Barbara George and Labelle; the Mighty Diamonds and Paul Simon have recorded at his Sansu Studio. Lee Dorsey's (1) hits were "Ya Ya" (1961) and "Working in the Coal Mine" (1966). Ernie K-Doe (5) recorded "Mother-in-Law" in 1961. Irma Thomas (4) was the first to record "Time Is on My Side," immediately covered by the Rolling Stones, and Larry Williams (7) hit with "Short Fat Fannie," "Bony Maronie" (1957) and "Dizzy Miss Lizzy" (1958).

1

2

3

6

4

5

7

99

1

2

3

4

5

✎ *Walking to New Orleans*

In 1957 Huey "Piano" Smith (8) and the Clowns—with singer Bobby Marchan (7)—had a hit with "Rocking Pneumonia and the Boogie Woogie Flu," followed in 1958 by "Don't You Just Know It" and "High Blood Pressure." The following year, their "Sea Cruise" became a hit for Frankie Ford (6), when the Clowns' vocals were replaced on the track by Ford's. By 1966, when Aaron Neville's (3) "Tell It like It Is" became a hit, he and his brothers had been recording and performing around New Orleans for a decade. Later, they toured as the Neville Brothers. Clarence "Frogman" Henry (1) earned his middle (nick)name from his 1956 R&B hit, "Ain't Got No Home," on which he used three different voices. Later hits included "But I Do" and "You Always Hurt the One You Love" (1961). Barbara George (4) recorded 1961's "I Know," pianist Jessie Hill (2) had a hit with "Ooh Poo Pah Doo," and bandleader Joe Jones (5) wrote and recorded "You Talk Too Much" in 1960.

6

7

8

⌁ *Southern Love*

The late-'50s Texas sound blended
country, pop and a heavier backbeat.
Dale Hawkins (2) hit in 1957 with
"Susie-Q," which featured James
Burton on lead guitar. Later singles
included "Class Cutter (Yeah Yeah)."
The Rhythm Orchids' (5) "Party
Doll" / "I'm Sticking with You"
(1957) was so successful that one
group member, Buddy Knox (3),
released "Party Doll" under his own
name and Jimmy Bowen (4), had the
flip side under his. Knox continued
to chart through the '60s with "Hula
Love," "Somebody Touched Me"
and "Lovey Dovey," among others.
Bowen went on to produce Frank
Sinatra and others. From Arkansas,
Ronnie Hawkins (1) recorded "Forty
Days," "Mary Lou" and "Who Do
You Love." He is known for hiring
the Band, who backed him for years
in Canada before joining Bob Dylan
in the mid-'60s.

3

4

5

4

〜 *Party Dolls*

The girl groups of the '50s were, for the most part, one-hit wonders, purveyors of novelty tunes, or both. The exception was the Chantels (2), five girls aged thirteen to sixteen, who recorded "Maybe" in 1958. Although they had only three more Top Forty hits, "Every Night (I Pray)," "Well, I Told You" and "Look in My Eyes" (1958-61), the Chantels are important because they were the first major girl group to feature a lead vocalist—in their case, Arlene Smith, one of rock & roll's best. The Bobbettes (1), who were younger than the Chantels, wrote and recorded "Mr. Lee" in 1957. The song was about their school principal, who returned as the subject of their 1960 flop sequel, "I Shot Mr. Lee." Subsequent singles included "Have Mercy Baby" (1960). The Shepherd Sisters' (3) "Alone (Why Must I Be Alone)" (1957) and the Poni-Tails' (4) "Born Too Late" (1958) were their only hits.

1

2

3

4

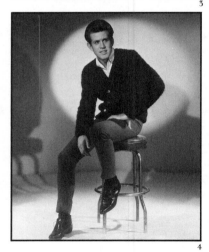

5

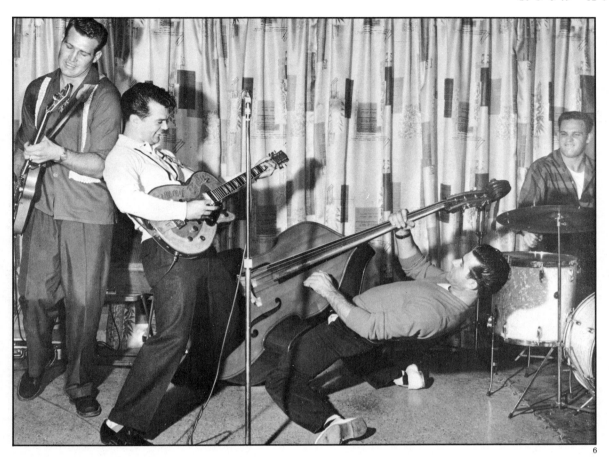

6

🎵 *His Master's Voice*

Before there were Elvis
impersonators, there were Elvis
soundalikes. Two contemporary
country stars made early hits in the
Presley style: Conway Twitty (6)
(born Harold Jenkins; 5, with Mamie
Van Doren) with 1958's "It's Only
Make Believe" and Terry Stafford
(4), who covered an Elvis LP cut,
"Suspicion," in 1964. Other careers
began with this form of flattery. Jack
Scott's (1, 2) first hit was the 1958
ballad "My True Love." Two years
later, Ray Smith (3) recorded a
remarkably accurate Sun-era-style
"That's All Right with Me." And
when Joe Dowell (7) covered Elvis's
"Wooden Heart" from the *G.I. Blues*
soundtrack, he learned the German
lyrics from the original. Ral Donner
(8) recorded "You Don't Know What
You've Got" and "Girl of My Best
Friend" (1961).

7

8

~ *Memories of El Monte*

As a writer, producer, bandleader, performer and talent scout, Johnny Otis did more than any other person to support R&B and early rock & roll. Otis was born John Veliotes to Greek-American parents in 1921. By the time he was in his teens, he had learned to play drums, piano and vibraphone, and had a reputation around the Bay Area as a swing musician. In 1948, he and his partner, Bardu Ali, opened the Barrelhouse Club in Watts. It became the center of Los Angeles's burgeoning R&B scene. In 1950 alone, Otis was responsible for seven R&B Top Ten hits. The next year, he discovered Jackie Wilson, Hank Ballard and Little Willie John in Detroit. In 1949, he discovered Little Esther Phillips (2), for whom he wrote "Double Crossing Blues," an R&B Number One in 1950. Several years later, he discovered Marie Adams and the Three Tons of Joy (1), who had a 1957 hit in England with "Ma, He's Making Eyes at Me." By the early '50s, he began touring with his R&B Caravan of Stars (3). Also pictured here are Otis with Little Arthur Matthews (5) and with the Dell-Vikings (4).

∿ *Memories of El Monte*

One of Otis's most successful protégées was Etta James (4), whom he discovered in San Francisco in the early '50s. In 1955, she recorded "Roll with Me, Henry," an R&B hit covered on the pop charts by Georgia Gibbs as "Dance with Me, Henry." It wasn't until the '60s that Etta hit her full stride. The Teen Queens (3), sisters Betty and Rosie Collins, hit with "Eddie My Love" in 1956. Mel Williams (1, left, with the Penguins) hit solo with "All thru the Night," and Bob (Relf) and Earl (Nelson) (2) had two pop singles, "Don't Ever Leave Me" and "Harlem Shuffle," in the early '60s. Don Julian and the Meadowlarks (5) hit with "Heaven and Paradise" in 1955.

〰 *Memories of El Monte*

Johnny Otis also discovered the Robins (2), who in 1950 provided the background vocals for Little Esther's "Double Crossing Blues." In 1955, they had a hit with "Smokey Joe's Cafe," and were signed by Atlantic Records. Robins Carl Gardner and Bobby Nunn and two new members, Billy Guy and Leon Hughes, became the Coasters (3; 6, with Dick Clark). Their six Top Ten hits included "Searchin'," "Charlie Brown" and "Poison Ivy." In 1957, Cornel Gunter of the Flairs (1) became the Coasters' second tenor. Singer Jesse Belvin (5) cowrote the Penguins' "Earth Angel" (1954), and his "Goodnight My Love" was Alan Freed's sign-off theme. Belvin had two pop singles months before he died in a car crash in 1960 at age twenty-six. Besides being great showmen, Don and Dewey (4, with Otis)—guitarist/violinist Don "Sugarcane" Harris and pianist Dewey Terry—were successful songwriters ("Justine," "Big Boy Pete").

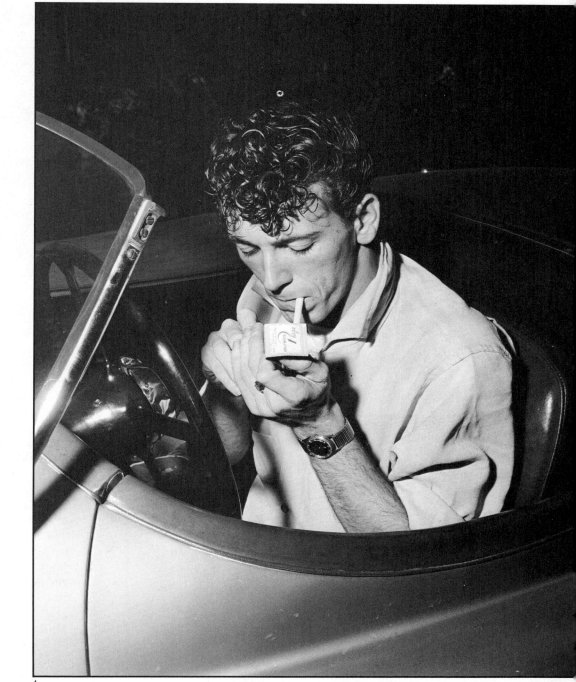

~~ *Race with the Devil*

Like his friend Eddie Cochran, Gene Vincent was a rougher, greasier sort of star. Vincent was born into a poor Virginia family; at age sixteen, he left home. Four years later, while serving in the navy, Vincent so seriously injured his leg in a motorcycle accident that he nearly lost it. It was to become the source of near intractable pain for the rest of his life. While recuperating, Vincent learned to play guitar. He also began performing on local country & western radio programs. A year later, he recorded "Be-Bop-A-Lula" with the Blue Caps (1, 3). Though he had only one more Top Twenty hit— "Lotta Lovin'" in 1957—his debut eventually sold over 9 million copies. In the next few years, he frequently toured England, where he was a tremendous star and became a trend-setter for the British teenage Teddy boys, as well as a major influence on the young Beatles. During a 1960 British tour, he was in the car crash that killed Eddie Cochran. Years of heavy drinking took their toll. In 1971, he died of a bleeding ulcer at age thirty- six.

4

1

~ *I'm Gonna Raise a Fuss*

During Eddie Cochran's short yet
brilliant career, he recorded
"Summertime Blues," "Somethin'
Else" and "C'mon Everybody," three
singles that summed up American
teen life better than other artists
have over a long career. In
Oklahoma, Cochran began his
career with an unrelated hillbilly
singer named Hank Cochran.
Falsely billed as the Cochran
Brothers (3, Eddie, left), they worked
together from 1954 to 1956 and cut a
few unsuccessful singles. Cochran
was a writer and session guitarist
before he released "Summertime
Blues" in 1958. That same year, he
hit with "Somethin' Else" and in
1959 with "C'mon Everybody." He
appeared with his friend Gene
Vincent in *The Girl Can't Help It*.
Like many '50s American rockers,
Cochran became more popular in
Britain. On April 17, 1960, while en
route to a London airport, Cochran
was killed in a car accident at age
twenty-one. His current British hit
was "Three Steps to Heaven." Here,
Cochran (5, right) is pictured with
Vincent and a fan.

2

3

4

5

ᴥ *Genius and Soul*

Ray Charles is the genius of soul—and just about every other form of music. Since his 1951 chart debut, Charles has recorded gospel, pop, jazz and country. In 1936, at age six, Ray Charles Robinson contracted glaucoma, which soon left him blind. He continued to study music—he plays virtually every instrument—until 1945, when he left school to join a dance band. He dropped his surname and two years later began singing. Initially attacked for making gospel songs like "Talkin' 'bout Jesus" rock in a secular style (as in "Talkin' 'bout You"), Charles became the master of fervent blues and call-and-response vocals, as he traded with the Raelettes on "I've Got a Woman" and "What'd I Say," his signature tune. His first pop Number One, 1960's "Georgia on My Mind," blended country & western with R&B and featured full strings. Then, and ever since, Charles simultaneously burned up the pop and R&B charts while recording classic jazz and country albums.

1

2

3

4

5

1

2

3

❧ *Do You Wanna Dance*

Thurston Harris (3), originally a member of the Lamplighters, was backed by the Sharps when he recorded his sole pop Top Ten hit, "Little Bitty Pretty One" (1957). "Do What You Did" and "Over and Over" followed in 1958. Billy Myles (2) had a hit with "The Joker (That's What They Call Me)," which he had written for the Mello-Kings, a group for whom he had earlier composed "Tonite Tonite." Bobby Freeman (1) was still in high school when he recorded "Do You Want to Dance" in 1958. Six years later, he had a pair of dance hits, "C'mon and Swim" and "S-W-I-M." Wilbert Harrison (4) had a hit with his version of Leiber and Stoller's "Kansas City" in 1959. Due to contractual litigation, a decade passed before he scored again. His hit, which he recorded as a one-man band, was "Let's Work Together," later covered by Canned Heat among others.

4

1

2

3

♫ *Do You Wanna Dance*

Chuck Willis was a leading black vocalist, songwriter and the king of the stroll. Willis, who wore turbans onstage to hide his premature balding, recorded "C.C. Rider" in 1957. The next year, after recording "What Am I Living For" and "Hang Up My Rock & Roll Shoes," he died in a car crash at age thirty. He is pictured here with guitarist Roy Gaines (4). Brook Benton (3) had over three dozen hits in a decade. He cowrote "Looking Back" for Nat "King" Cole and "A Lover's Question" for Clyde McPhatter. In addition to his solo hits ("It's Just a Matter of Time," 1959; "The Boll Weevil Song," 1961), he recorded two hit duets with Dinah Washington in 1960. His biggest hit was 1970's "Rainy Night in Georgia." Tommy Edwards (5) recorded "It's All in the Game" in 1951, but it didn't become a hit until seven years later. Sonny Knight's (2) 1956 hit was "Confidential." In the '70s, he wrote *The Day the Music Died*. Ed Townsend (1) studied law before recording "For Your Love" in 1958.

4

5

♫ *Love Is Strange*

Mickey and Sylvia were Mickey "Guitar" Baker and Sylvia Vanderpool Robinson (2, 6). The duo met in 1955 when Mickey was hired to teach Sylvia guitar. Each had recorded solo before, she as Little Sylvia (4), and they released five singles before "Love Is Strange" became a hit in 1956. They continued to chart through 1961, but never with the same results. Mickey, a renowned blues guitarist, moved to Europe, and Sylvia founded All-Platinum and Sugar Hill Records. In 1973, she had a huge disco hit with "Pillow Talk." Gene (Forrest) and Eunice (Levy) (5) had two major hits, "Koko Mo" (1955) and "Poco Loco" (1959), before disappearing from the charts. Johnnie and Joe (3) hit with "Over the Mountain; Across the Sea" in 1957. Tarheel Slim and Little Ann (1) recorded the unbelievably melodramatic tale of adultery and murder, "Two-Time Loser."

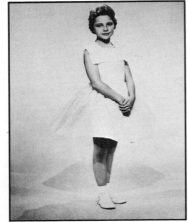

♪ *Sweet Nothin's*

Connie Francis and Brenda Lee were the two most popular female singers of the '50s. From novelty songs to standards, both made classic hits with their big, unique and dramatic voices. At nineteen, Connie Francis (1, 3, 5) recorded "Who's Sorry Now," a song from 1923. From serious ballads ("My Happiness," "Where the Boys Are") to uptempo singles ("Everybody's Somebody's Fool," "My Heart Has a Mind of Its Own") and rocking novelties like "Lipstick on Your Collar," Connie had over fifty chart singles. Brenda Lee (2, 4, 6) began singing professionally at seven. Born Brenda Mae Tarpley, she was only thirteen when she recorded her second chart hit, 1957's "Dynamite"; thereafter, she was known as Little Miss Dynamite. Her style was more explosive than Francis's, and her hits—"Sweet Nothin's," "I'm Sorry," "Emotions," "Dum Dum," "Break It to Me Gently," "All Alone Am I"—continued into 1966. Brenda then returned to her roots, churning out country hits.

4

5

6

4

~ *Teenagers in Love*

Dion DiMucci was the most soulful of all white singers, a teen idol with guts. Dion (4) began singing when he was five. In 1958, he formed the Belmonts (2, 3)—Fred Milano, Angelo D'Aleo and Carlo Mastrangelo—whom he named after Belmont Avenue in the Bronx. The same year, the group recorded "I Wonder Why." Their six other hit singles included "A Teenager in Love" and "Where or When" (1959). In 1960, Dion and the Belmonts went their separate ways. The Belmonts (1, with Dick Clark) continued to record through 1963. Dion released "A Lonely Teenager" at the end of 1960 and became even bigger. Over the next three years, he charted eight Top Ten singles: "Runaround Sue," about the girl he later married (1961), "The Wanderer," "Lovers Who Wander," "Little Diane," "Love Came to Me" (1962), "Ruby Baby," "Donna the Prima Donna" and "Drip Drop" (1963). In 1968, he returned with "Abraham, Martin and John."

♪ *Teen Beats*

Fifties instrumental hits were, more often than not, either one-shots or brief excursions onto the pop charts by artists better known in other fields. Perez Prado (3) had two Number One hits, "Cherry Pink and Apple Blossom White" (1955) and "Patricia" (1958). Noble "Thin Man" Watts's (1) hit was 1957's "Hard Times (the Slop)." Bill Doggett (2), a former bandleader, hit in 1956 with "Honky Tonk." Doc Bagby (4) appeared on the charts with "Dumplin's." Sandy Nelson (6), who drummed on the Teddy Bears' "To Know Him Is to Love Him," had a million-seller with "Teen Beat" in 1959. During late 1958, Cozy Cole (7) hit three times in four months: "Topsy I," "Topsy II" and "Turvy II." Preston Epps (8) did "Bongo Rock" in 1959. In 1957, Bill Justis (5) hit with "Raunchy."

4

6

7

5

8

131

1

2

132

⌒ *Teen Beats*

In 1958, Link Wray, with his group
the Wraymen (1), made the first
record that intentionally included
guitar distortion, "Rumble." Legend
has it that Wray (2) produced the
sound by piercing his amplifier with
a pencil. Due to its ominous tone
and title, "Rumble" was also widely
associated with juvenile delinquency,
"rumble" being slang for a street-
gang fight. His later hits included
"Raw Hide" (1959) and "Jack the
Ripper" (1963). Over the years Wray
has rerecorded "Rumble" several
times. In 1977, he teamed up with
rockabilly revivalist Robert Gordon.
Santo and Johnny (3), the Farina
brothers, had hits with "Sleep Walk"
(1959) and "Caravan" (1960), the
only steel-guitar pop hits of the '50s.
Dave "Baby" Cortez (4) was
a singer/pianist whose hits, "The
Happy Organ" (1959) and "Rinky
Dink" (1962), featured him on organ.

4

3

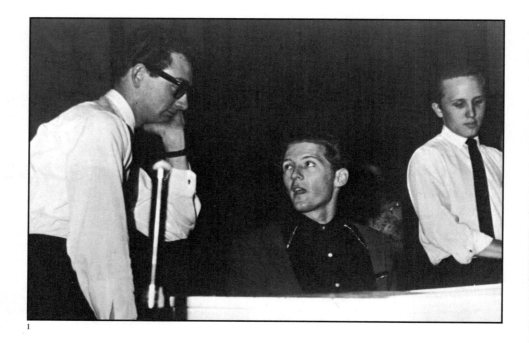

1

2

♫ *Bigger than a Cadillac*

During the two short years he recorded his hits, Buddy Holly (2), wrote and sang classic songs that are more influential today than they were in his lifetime. Charles Hardin Holley grew up in Lubbock, Texas, where he learned to play guitar and started performing. After an unsuccessful two-year stint in a duo with Bob Montgomery, he signed to Decca and cut several tunes with Sonny Curtis and Jerry Allison. He moved to Brunswick, and later formed the Crickets with Allison and Joe Mauldin. On February 25, 1957, they drove to Clovis, New Mexico, where they recorded with producer Norman Petty in his studio. During 1957, Holly and the Crickets released the Number One "That'll Be the Day," plus two Top Tens— "Peggy Sue" and "Oh Boy." Despite an auspicious start, in 1958 Holly had but two Top Thirty singles, "Maybe Baby" and "Think It Over." Other releases from that year were "Early in the Morning," "Rave On" and "Fool's Paradise." Holly is pictured here (1, left) with Jerry Lee Lewis.

3

4

1

2

3

4

〜 *Bigger than a Cadillac*

By the fall of 1958, Holly was recording solo. He'd left the Crickets (1, 5) and Petty (2), married and moved to Greenwich Village. Though still writing and recording, he seemed to have lost direction. He was considering recording a tribute LP to Ray Charles, according to friend Snuff Garrett. His latest hit, "Heartbeat," had just squeaked onto the charts and so, reluctantly, he joined a package tour with the Big Bopper (J. P. Richardson) (6) and Ritchie Valens (4). The three died on February 3, 1959, when their small chartered plane crashed. In March, Tommy Dee (3) recorded "Three Stars," a tribute to Holly, Richardson and Valens, in Petty's studio.

5

6

Part II   **OSMOSIS**

Late '50s to Mid-'60s

3

✎ *Soul Man*

Sam Cooke was the first major gospel singer to meld sexuality and sophistication in an early form of soul. The son of a Baptist minister, Cooke (3) grew up in Chicago, where, from age nine, he sang professionally with three of his siblings as the Singing Children. He was fifteen when he joined the Soul Stirrers, an established gospel quintet that had pioneered the single-lead-with-group-background vocal arrangements that would permanently change gospel music. Soon after leaving the Soul Stirrers (4, Cooke on left), he had his only Number One hit, "You Send Me." In 1958, Cooke went on tour with another gospel group, the Pilgrim Travelers, which included Lou Rawls (1, Rawls second from right); Rawls's hits included "Love Is a Hurtin' Thing" in 1966. Best friends, Cooke and Rawls often sang uncredited on each other's records. In fact, Rawls (2) provided the second, "response" vocal on Cooke's 1962 hit "Bring It On Home to Me."

4

1

〜 *Soul Man*

From 1957 until his death in December 1964, Cooke had twenty-nine Top Forty hits, including "Wonderful World," "Chain Gang" (1960), "Cupid" (1961), "Twistin' the Night Away," "Having a Party" (1962) and "Shake" (1965), most of which were produced by Hugo Peretti and Luigi Creatore (4).

2

3

Cooke was also one of the first black entrepreneurs in music; he owned the Sar label and discovered and produced the Sims Twins ("Soothe Me," 1961) and Johnnie Taylor, who had replaced Cooke in the Soul Stirrers and later hit in 1968 with "Who's Making Love" and in 1976 with "Disco Lady." Cooke also discovered and produced two major hits with the Valentinos (a group featuring Bobby Womack and his brothers), "Lookin' for a Love" (1962) and "It's All Over Now" (1964). He is pictured here in the studio with Cassius Clay (5). Cooke was rightfully acknowledged as the Father of Soul. He was shot to death in a Los Angeles motel on December 11, 1964; he was twenty-nine years old. His last recording was "A Change Is Gonna Come."

4

5

♪ *The Bird's the Word*

Many early white rock groups were one-hit wonders. Long Island's the Bell Notes (2) had a single Top Twenty hit, "I've Had It" (1959), as did the Dartells (4) ("Hot Pastrami," 1963) and the Rivieras (5) ("California Sun," 1964). The Fleetwoods (6), a vocal trio, wrote a pair of 1959 Number Ones, "Come Softly to Me" and "Mr. Blue." They continued to chart through 1963. The Trashmen's (3) 1963 novelty hit, "Surfin' Bird," made another group, the Rivingtons, money after they proved that the Trashmen had plagiarized their hits, "Papa Oom Mow Mow" and "The Bird's the Word." The longest-lived of these early groups were the Fireballs (1), an instrumental group with several hits, including "Torquay" (1959) and "Bulldog" (1960). Later joined by pianist/vocalist Jimmy Gilmer, they hit Number One with "Sugar Shack" in 1963. Gilmer went solo, and the Fireballs returned in 1968 with "Bottle of Wine."

1

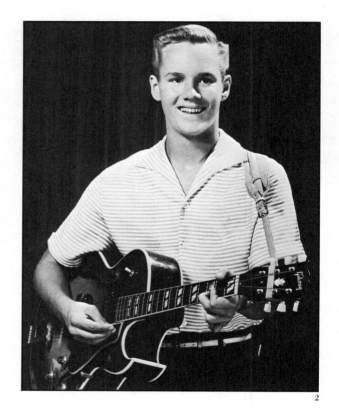

2

♒ *Somethin' Else*

J. P. Richardson (the Big Bopper) wrote and sang the background vocals on Johnny Preston's (3) 1959 Number One, "Running Bear." Preston's other hits included "Cradle of Love," "Feel So Fine" (1960), "Leave My Kitten Alone" and "Free Me" (1961). In the '70s, Anita Bryant (6) rose to fame as an evangelical antigay crusader, but in the late '50s she'd been a popular singer with such hits as "Til There Was You," "Paper Roses" and "In My Little Corner of the World" (1959-60). Rosie (of the Originals) Hamlin (5) recorded 1960's "Angel Baby," notable for its appalling but effective sax solo. Cathy Jean (4) and the Roommates' vocals epitomized prepubescent pop. Their 1961 hit was "Please Love Me Forever." Mitchell Torok's (1) 1959 hit, "Caribbean," featured his rockin' fiddle against a barrelhouse piano. And Robin Luke (2), a Hawaiian Buddy Holly soundalike, scored with 1958's "Susie Darlin'."

3

4

5

6

1

2

3

◜ *Dream Lover*

Bobby Darin (1, 3, 4) was one of the few '50s teen idols to make the transition into mainstream pop. Born Walden Robert Cassotto, Darin was raised in the Bronx by his widowed mother. In his teens, he accidentally overheard his mother and his doctor discuss his bad heart and the probability that he would not live to age twenty. Between then and his death at thirty-seven, Darin became ambition personified; he once claimed he would be bigger than Sinatra. He was twenty-two when "Splish Splash" hit. Several typically teen singles ("Queen of the Hop," "Dream Lover") followed before "Mack the Knife," his only Number One, in 1959. The next year, he made his movie debut in *Come September* and later wed his costar, Sandra Dee. He earned an Oscar nomination for best supporting actor in *Capt. Newman, M.D.* In 1966, he made a rock comeback with "If I Were a Carpenter," his last Top Ten hit. He died in 1973 during open-heart surgery in Los Angeles. He is pictured here with Jo Ann Campbell (2), Fabian (5) and King Curtis (6).

4

5

6

4

5

🎵 *Just a Dream*

Of the dozens of musicians and
singers to emerge from New
Orleans in the '50s, Jimmy Clanton
has the rare distinction of being the
Crescent City's only bona fide teen
idol. Clanton was discovered by
legendary local producer Cosimo
Matassa in 1958. Later that year he
had his first hit, "Just a Dream."
Subsequent hits included "A Letter
to an Angel," "A Part of Me," "My
Own True Love," "Go, Jimmy, Go,"
"Another Sleepless Night" and, in
1962, his last big one, "Venus in Blue
Jeans." Groomed for teen stardom,
he also appeared in *Go, Johnny, Go*,
with Ritchie Valens (4).

❧ *Teenage Idols*

Movie actors and television stars have regularly attempted recording careers with varying degrees of success. In 1961, just one year after George Burns took her to Las Vegas, Ann-Margret (Olson) (1) had a hit with "I Just Don't Understand." Sal Mineo (3) charted the first of six pop singles, "Start Movin' (in My Direction)" in 1957. Mineo, who hailed from the Bronx, was actually a decent singer, and, later that year, he hit again with "Lasting Love." Fess Parker (2) had one of 1955's biggest-selling singles, "The Ballad of Davy Crockett." Parker, who played Davy in the movie *Davy* *Crockett*, also spearheaded the coonskin cap craze, and the song itself—in a number of versions—sold over 18 million copies worldwide. Tab Hunter (4, right) (born Arthur Kelm) had seven chart singles, including the 1957 Number One "Young Love." Hunter, who sang even worse than he acted, followed it with "(I'll Be with You in) Apple Blossom Time" two years later.

4

❧ *Teenage Idols*

Ricky Nelson was the first video star; from 1957 until 1966, every weekly episode of his family's television series ended with him singing his latest tune, occasionally joined by acts like the Four Preps (5). As a result, Nelson had thirty-five Top Forty hits, including "Poor Little Fool," "It's Late," "Travelin' Man," "Hello Mary Lou" and "Fools Rush In." He recorded "A Teenager's Romance" after his date, an Elvis Presley fan, teased him about her idol. The week Nelson turned seventeen in 1957, his first single, "I'm Walking" / "A Teenager's Romance," hit the chart, and before long he became a teen idol. His backup band (4) featured James Burton on guitar (right) and Joe Osborne on bass (left). In 1972, he had a Top Ten hit with "Garden Party," an unsentimental rejection of the '50s nostalgia craze he, in part, inspired.

3

4

5

6

5

🎵 *Guitar Man*

Duane Eddy was the first rock-era instrumentalist to become a pop star. He was the originator of the "twangy" guitar sound that influenced the Shadows and the Ventures, among others. Eddy grew up in Phoenix, where he quit school at age sixteen to perform. In 1955, he and guitarist Al Casey formed the Rebels (5), and three years later Eddy had his first big hit, "Rebel-'Rouser." Before 1965, he had nineteen more hits, including

"Cannonball" (1958), "Forty Miles of Bad Road," "Some Kinda Earthquake" (1959) and "Because They're Young" (1960). From 1966 to 1969, he was married to Jessi Colter. Eddy continues to tour, primarily in England where he is still a star. He is pictured with Lester Sill (4, left) and Dick Clark (second from left).

♫ *Crossfire*

The late '50s and early '60s saw
several hits by saxophone-led
instrumental groups. The Royal
Teens (5) recorded "Short Shorts,"
which did have a few lyrics. In the
group were future Four Seasons
member/writer/producer Bob
Gaudio and Al Kooper. The Wailers
(3) hit with "Tall Cool One" in 1959;
the song recharted in 1964. The
Viscounts' (6) "Harlem Nocturne"
also charted twice, in 1959 and in
1965. The two most successful
groups were Johnny and the
Hurricanes and the Champs. Led by
sax player Johnny Paris (2), the
Hurricanes (1) had three 1959 hits,
"Crossfire," "Red River Rock" and
"Reveille Rock." Their last big hit,
"Beatnik Fly," came in 1960. The
Champs (4) began their four-year
string of hits with the Number One
"Tequila" in 1958. All West Coast
sessionmen, the Champs
experienced constant personnel
changes. This latter-day lineup (7)
included Glen Campbell (top, right),
Jimmy Seals (bottom, right) and
Dash Crofts (top, middle).

5

6

7

4

5

ᕈᐧ *Puppy Love*

Singer Paul Anka and ex-
Mouseketeer Annette Funicello
were the perfect teen-dream couple:
he was a singing idol, she a bosomy
aspiring actress. When Anka was
fifteen, he recorded his first Number
One single, "Diana," about his crush
on an older woman. Unlike other
heartthrobs, Anka wrote his own
material, much of it filled with polite
teen *angst*, heartfelt, but nothing to
leave home about. "Lonely Boy,"
"Put Your Head on My Shoulder"
and "Puppy Love" (written for
girlfriend Annette) were true teen
fare. Later, he wrote Tom Jones's
"She's a Lady," Sinatra's "My Way"
and the theme for *The Tonight
Show*. Annette too had a recording
career, more novelty oriented and
shorter lasting. Her biggest hit was
1959's "Tall Paul." Annette acted in a
series of beach-blanket-bimbo
movies.

6

161

1

2

3

4

5

∿ *Land of 1000 Dances*

Although Philadelphia is remembered as the home of *American Bandstand* and teen idols, other rock & rollers also emerged from the "City of Brotherly Love." Former chicken plucker Ernest Evans, who changed his name to Chubby Checker (5), had a hit with Hank Ballard's "The Twist" in 1960. Over the next five years, he recorded a series of dance-craze hits, including "Pony Time," "The Fly," "Slow Twistin'," "Limbo Rock" and "Popeye the Hitchhiker." The Dovells (4) had been a doo-wop group called the Cashmeres. With lead singer Len Barry ("1-2-3"), they recorded "Bristol Stomp" (1961) and "You Can't Sit Down" (1963). Frankie Avalon (born Avallone) (2, 3), a child prodigy trumpeter, was eighteen when his "Dede Dinah" hit the Top Ten. Subsequent hits included "Ginger Bread," "Venus" and "Why" (1958-60). He later made a series of beach-blanket movies with Annette (1), and, in 1976, charted with a disco remake of "Venus."

5

4

❧ *Land of 1000 Dances*

Fabian (Forte) (1, 3) was yet another
teen idol. He was only sixteen when
he charted seven singles in 1959,
including "Turn Me Loose," "Tiger"
and "Hound Dog Man." Fabian is
pictured here with actress Tuesday
Weld (2). Danny and the Juniors' (6)
two biggest hits—"At the Hop" (1957)
and "Rock and Roll Is Here to Stay"
(1958)—are rock anthems. Lead
singer Danny Rapp (far right)
committed suicide on April 5, 1983,
at forty-one. Freddy "Boom Boom"
Cannon's (4) first hit, 1959's
"Tallahassee Lassie," was written
with his mom. He made the Top Ten
again that year with "Way Down
Yonder in New Orleans" and three
years later with Chuck Barris's
"Palisades Park." Dicky Doo (Gerry
Granahan) and the Don'ts' (5) two
1958 hits were "Click-Clack" and
"Nee Nee Na Na Na Na Nu Nu."

6

1 6 5

1

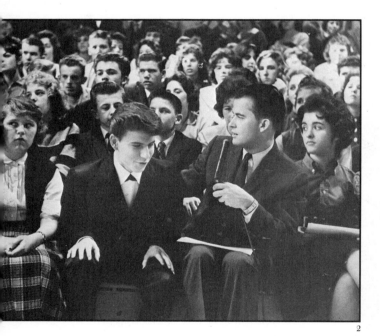

2

3

↝ *Land of 1000 Dances*

Bobby Rydell (4) had played drums in Rocco and His Saints with Frankie Avalon before starting his own solo career. Between 1959 and 1965, he charted twenty-nine singles, including "Kissin' Time," "Sway," "Swingin' School," "Wild One," "Volare " and "Forget Him." In 1961 he recorded "Jingle Bell Rock" with Chubby Checker. He was Ann-Margret's boyfriend Hugo Peabody in *Bye Bye Birdie.* He is pictured here with Annette (1) and Dick Clark (2). Dione LaRue began singing as Dee Dee Sharp (5) after answering a newspaper ad placed by Cameo-Parkway Records. After doing background vocals on some Chubby Checker hits, she charted several of her own, including 1962's "Slow Twistin'," "Mashed Potato Time," "Gravy (for My Mashed Potatoes)" and "Ride!" Jodie Sands's (6) 1957 hit single was "With All My Heart." Billy Ford's Thunderbirds (3) had two hits as Billy & Lillie (named for the two lead singers; top, middle)—"Lucky Ladybug" and "La-Dee-Dah."

4

5

6

🎵 *Lightnin' Strikes*

Joey Dee and the Starliters (4, 5) had long been the house band at New York's Peppermint Lounge when their "Peppermint Twist" went to Number One in 1961. Other hits included 1962's "Hey Let's Twist" and a cover of the Isleys' "Shout." The Starliters' ever-changing lineup at one time included three of the original Rascals—Felix Cavaliere, Gene Cornish and Eddie Brigati. Lou Christie's (2) wild falsetto graced his "The Gypsy Cried," "Two Faces Have I" (1963), "Lightnin' Strikes " and "Rhapsody in the Rain" (1966), the last of which was banned in Britain because of its sexually explicit lyrics. Bobby Comstock (3) and the Counts recorded "Tennessee Waltz" (1959) and "Let's Stomp" (1963). Paul Evans's Top Ten hits were "Seven Little Girls Sitting in the Back Seat" (1959) and "Happy-Go-Lucky Me" (1960). He is seen here with his wife (1).

4

5

❧ *A Star Is Born*

Television and film stars continued
to venture into recording. Edd
Byrnes (3), Kookie of *77 Sunset Strip*,
went Top Ten in 1959 with "Kookie,
Kookie (Lend Me Your Comb),"
which featured Connie Stevens (2).
Stevens, who played Cricket on
Hawaiian Eye, had her own hit the
next year, "Sixteen Reasons." Eddie
Hodges (4) was fourteen when he
recorded "I'm Gonna Knock on Your
Door" in 1961. His next hit was 1962's
"(Girls, Girls, Girls) Made to Love."
Johnny Crawford (5), the Rifleman's
son Mark, recorded 1962's "Cindy's
Birthday" and "Rumors." Shelley
Fabares (with Fabian, 1) of *The
Donna Reed Show* went to Number
One with "Johnny Angel." Hayley
Mills (7), fifteen-year-old actress
daughter of British actor John Mills,
recorded "Let's Get Together" and
"Johnny Jingo" (1961-62). Another
film star, James Darren (8), had two
Top Tens, "Goodbye Cruel World"
and "Her Royal Majesty" (1961-62).
Actress Sandra Dee (6) never made
the charts, but her husband Bobby
Darin did.

1

2

3

4

5

7

6

8

✒︎ *Come Back When You Grow Up*

Robert Velline was only fifteen years old when he and his group, the Shadows, were hired to sub for the late Buddy Holly at a Mason City, Iowa, show just days after Holly's death. Within the year, "Suzie Baby" —the only record Vee would make with the Shadows (5), which then included his brother—was a minor national hit. From there, Vee became one of the most successful and longest-lived teen superstars, with such hits as "Rubber Ball," "Devil or Angel" (1960), the Number One "Take Good Care of My Baby," "Run to Him" (1961), "Please Don't Ask about Barbara" (1962), "The Night Has a Thousand Eyes," "Charms" (1963) and "Come Back When You Grow Up" (1967). In 1962, he recorded *Bobby Vee Meets the Crickets*, an album tribute to Holly. In 1972 a bearded Velline attempted a rock comeback under his own name with *Nothin' like a Sunny Day*.

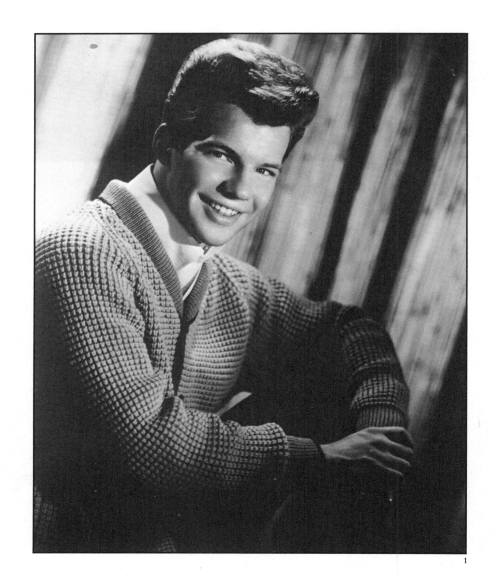

1

2

3

4

5

1

3

4

2

♫ *Teen Angels*

Underage death was a recurring theme in early-'60s teen ballads. In Ray Peterson's (5) "Tell Laura I Love Her" (1960), the song's hero dies in an auto race he'd entered to raise the cash for a wedding ring. The heroine of Mark Dinning's (4) 1960 "Teen Angel" gets in the way of a speeding train while frantically searching her stalled car for her boyfriend's high-school ring. In J. Frank Wilson and the Cavaliers' (1) 1964 hit "Last Kiss," the singer's date is accidentally run over by his car. She dies just after J. Frank plants a last kiss on her lips. Jimmy Cross (3) wasn't content to let romance end with mere mortality: "I Want My Baby Back," he laments, and proceeds to dig up her coffin and climb inside her room with no view. And Jody Reynolds (2) went Top Five with the suicide dirge "Endless Sleep."

5

1

2

4

3

∿ *Just a Little Bit Longer*

Although doo-wop's heyday was the
early to mid-'50s, several groups
carried the style into the '60s. The
Cleftones (7), whose earlier hits
included "You Baby You" (1956), had
a pair of 1961 hits, "Heart and Soul"
and "For Sentimental Reasons."
James "Shep" Sheppard, the lead
singer for the Heartbeats between
1956 and 1958, had a Number Two
hit in 1961 with the Limelites
(6), "Daddy's Home." The
Edsels (3) hit locally in Baltimore
with "Rama Lama Ding Dong."
Three years later, in 1961, "Rama
Lama Ding Dong" became a
national hit in the wake of the
Marcels' similar sounding "Blue
Moon." Maurice Williams—who had
written and recorded "Little
Darlin'" with the Gladiolas in 1957—
and the Zodiacs (2) hit Number One
in 1960 with "Stay," recently
recorded by Bruce Springsteen with
Jackson Browne. The Shells (5) are
best known for "Baby Oh Baby" and
"Never Never" (1961). The Jive
Five's (4) hits included "My True
Story" and "No Not Again." Ronnie
(Goodson) and the Hi-Lites (1)
recorded their only hit, "I Wish
That We Were Married," in 1962.
Later singles included 1965's "I'm
a Happy Man."

1

2 3 4

5

6

7

8

♪ *Just a Little Bit Longer*

Named after the group members' hairstyle, the Marcels (8) had three hits in 1961 with comedic versions of standards: "Blue Moon," "Summertime" and "Heartaches." The Impalas (1) were one of a few interracial groups. Their hit was 1959's "Sorry (I Ran All the Way Home)." Many of the groups who extended the black doo-wop style were, unlike its originators, white. The Fireflies (2), whose 1959 hit was "You Were Mine," featured Ritchie Adams, composer of Bobby Lewis's "Tossin' and Turnin'." Randy and the Rainbows' (6) biggest hit was 1963's "Denise." The Skyliners' (5) hits were: "Since I Don't Have You," "This I Swear" (1959) and "Pennies from Heaven" (1960). Many others were classic one-shot wonders: The Mello-Kings' (7) "Tonite Tonite" charted twice, in 1957 and 1961, the Elegants (3) had a Number One hit in 1958 with "Little Star," and the Earls (4) made their sole chart appearance with "Remember Then" in 1962.

1

2

~ *Just a Little Bit Longer*

As doo-wop moved into the '60s, emphasis shifted from romantic ballads to virtually everything, ranging from the sickly sweet to the comedic absurd. In the former category were Ruby and the Romantics (2). Originally an all-male quartet, the group added lead singer Ruby Nash in 1962. The following year, they had a pair of hits, "Our Day Will Come" and "My Summer Love." The Tymes (1), from Philadelphia, also had two 1963 hits, "So Much in Love" and "Wonderful! Wonderful!" The Olympics (3), who formed in high school, had several hits, including "Western Movies" (1958), "Shimmy like Kate" and "Dance by the Light of the Moon" (1960). The Rivingtons' (4) two totally crazed early-'60s hits, "Papa Oom Mow Mow" and "The Bird's the Word" "inspired" the Trashmen's "Surfin' Bird."

3

4

♪ *Stairway to Heaven*

In the late '50s, the Brill Buiding—
1619 Broadway—housed young
songwriters Jeff Barry and Ellie
Greenwich (2), Carole King and
Gerry Goffin (1), Neil Sedaka (3) and
Tony Orlando (4). Barry and
Greenwich wrote innumerable hits,
including "Do Doo Ron Ron" (the
Crystals). Tony Orlando, then
sixteen, cowrote with Carole King
and Gerry Goffin "Halfway to
Paradise," which along with "Bless
You" were his 1961 hits. Goffin and
King also wrote tons of hits: "Will
You Love Me Tomorrow" (the
Shirelles) and "Up on the Roof" (the
Drifters). Neil Sedaka, a classical
pianist, wrote "Stupid Cupid"
(Connie Francis) and had his own
hits with "Calendar Girl," "Happy
Birthday, Sweet Sixteen" and
"Breaking Up Is Hard to Do" in the
early '60s. Pictured here (5) on
American Bandstand are, left to
right, announcer Charlie O'Donnell,
Dick Clark, Sedaka, Freddy Cannon,
Bobby Rydell, Chubby Checker.

1

2

1

2

184

〜 *Girls Talk*

The Angels (1, 2) were one of the first white girl groups. Formed in New Jersey, the Angels—sisters Barbara and Jiggs Allbut and Peggy Santiglia—had several hits, including "'Til" (1961), "Cry Baby Cry" (1962) and the Number One "My Boyfriend's Back" two years later. The Shangri-Las (4) were sisters Mary and Betty Weiss and twins Mary Ann and Marge Ganser. Produced by George "Shadow" Morton, the quartet (only three of whom toured), sang dramatic narrative tunes full of teen *angst*. Their biggest hits included "Remember (Walkin' in the Sand)," the Number One "Leader of the Pack," "Give Him a Great Big Kiss" (1964),"Give Us Your Blessings" and "I Can Never Go Home Anymore" (1965). The next year they disbanded. Also pictured, the Devonnes (3).

4

5

✍ *Girls Talk*

One of the most successful girl groups, the Shirelles (4) (named after lead singer Shirley Alston) was one of the few to write their own hits. Their top singles included "I Met Him on a Sunday" (1958), "Tonight's the Night" (1960), a cover of the Five Royales' "Dedicated to the One I Love," "Mama Said" (1961), a pair of Number Ones, "Will You Love Me Tomorrow" (1960) and "Soldier Boy" (1962), and "Foolish Little Girl" (1963). They are pictured here in the studio with Brooks Arthur (5). The Ad-Libs (2), were four men and a female lead singer, Mary Ann Thomas; they had the perfect girl-group sound with their only Top Ten hit, "The Boy from New York City." The Blue-Belles' (3)—lead singer Patti LaBelle (top middle), Nona Hendryx, Sarah Dash and Cindy Birdsong—biggest hit was 1962's "I Sold My Heart to the Junkman." In 1967, Birdsong replaced Florence Ballard in the Supremes. Four years later the trio reemerged as Labelle with a self-titled debut LP and *It's Gonna Take a Miracle* with Laura Nyro. Their 1975 disco smash was "Lady Marmalade." The Orlons (1) had hits with "The Wah Watusi" and "Not Me" (1962-63).

〜 *Girls Talk*

Another sexually integrated girl group was the Sensations (3); three male singers and lead vocalist Yvonne Baker. Their sole hit was 1962's "Let Me In." The Essex (6) were three marines, two men and Anita Humes. Their biggest single, "Easier Said than Done," hit Number One in 1963. The Sherrys (2) had one hit, 1962's "Pop Pop Pop-Pie." The Dixiebelles' (4) "(Down at) Papa Joe's" is a New Orleans classic that was recorded phonetically by Nashville session singers. Joe Jones, who wrote "You Talk Too Much," discovered the Dixie Cups (1). The trio's hits included "People Say" and "Chapel of Love," a Number One in 1964 that Phil Spector, Jeff Barry and Ellie Greenwich had written for the Ronettes. The Toys' (5) 1965 hit, "A Lover's Concerto," was based on Bach's Minuet in G. Their followups include "Attack" (1965).

1

2

3

4

5

6

1

2

3

4

〜 *Girls Talk*

One of the most popular girl groups, the Chiffons (6) with lead singer Judy Craig, had a Number One hit in 1963, "He's So Fine." The tune became the subject of a plagiarism suit in 1976, six years after George Harrison took the melody of it to Number One as "My Sweet Lord." Their last Top Ten hit was "Sweet Talkin' Guy" (1966). They are pictured here in the studio with Brooks Arthur (4). The Cookies (5) were studio singers for Neil Sedaka, Carole King and Little Eva. Their two hits were "Chains" (1962) and "Don't Say Nothin' Bad (about My Baby)" (1963). Many girl groups were one-hit wonders, such as Baby Jane and the Rockabyes (1), with "How Much Is That Doggie in the Window," an expert copy of Bob B. Soxx and the Blue Jeans "Zip-A-Dee Doo-Dah." The Secrets (2) recorded "The Boy Next Door" in 1963. The Jelly Beans' (3) two 1964 singles were "I Wanna Love Him So Bad" and "Baby Be Mine."

5

6

♫ *Girls Talk*

The Raindrops (1) were a studio group consisting of producers Jeff Barry (right) and Ellie Greenwich (middle), who had two 1963 hits, "What a Guy" and "The Kind of Boy You Can't Forget." Live, the Raindrops were a trio: Greenwich and two other women. The Blossoms (3) featured lead singer Darlene Love. Their 1961 single was "Son-In-Law," and they appeared regularly on *Shindig!* backing other guests. The Exciters' (7) two biggest releases were "Tell Him" and "He's Got the Power" (1963). The Murmaids' (2) "Popsicles and Icicles" (1963) was written by David Gates of Bread. Reparata (Mary Aiese) and the Delrons' (5) "Whenever a Teenager Cries" (1965) was their biggest U.S. hit. They later became Lady Flash. The Pixies Three's (4) "Birthday Party" hit in 1963, the same year the Caravelles (6) scored with "You Don't Have to Be a Baby to Cry."

1

2

3

4

5

6

7

2

1

∿ *Half Heaven, Half Heartache*

Roy Orbison, Del Shannon and Gene Pitney were the three most distinctive white male vocalists of the early '60s. Orbison (3, 4), was a successful songwriter (the Everly Brothers' "Claudette"). After his 1956 hit, "Ooby Dooby," subsequent hard-rock singles faltered. Orbison hit his stride in 1960 after signing to Monument Records and releasing "Only the Lonely," a dramatic ballad that set the tone for most of his other hits, including "Running Scared," "In Dreams" and the uptempo "Oh, Pretty Woman" (1961-64). Del Shannon (5) (Charles Westover) began recording in 1961 at age twenty-two. He hit Number One that year with "Runaway," featuring the Musitron, an early keyboard synthesizer; "Hats off to Larry" and "Keep Searchin'" followed. Before Gene Pitney (1, 2) released his debut single, "(I Wanna) Love My Life Away," in 1961, he wrote "He's a Rebel" and "Hello Mary Lou." Later singles included "Town without Pity" (1962) and "It Hurts to Be in Love" (1964). Pitney later recorded with George Jones.

3

4

5

1

∿ *He's a Rebel*

Producer Phil Spector began his career as a member of the Teddy Bears (4, left to right: Spector, Annette Bard, Marshall Lieb). In 1958, they recorded his "To Know Him Is to Love Him." After a followup flopped, the group disbanded. In 1960, Spector became a production assistant for, among others, Leiber and Stoller. Early projects included cowriting and coproducing Ben E. King's 1960 solo debut, "Spanish Harlem," and producing Ray Peterson's (2) "Corinna Corinna," Gene Pitney's "Every Breath I Take," Curtis Lee's (3) "Pretty Little Angel Eyes" and the Paris Sisters' (5) "I Love How You Love Me" (1961). In 1961, he and Lester Sill formed Philles Records; within three years, Spector had produced twenty smash hits and become a twenty-year-old millionaire. Here he is in the studio with engineer Brooks Arthur (1, Spector, middle; Arthur, right).

4

2

3

5

4

3

〜 *He's a Rebel*

The Ronettes (2, 3)—sisters Ronnie
and Estelle Bennett and their cousin
Nedra Talley—began performing
together in 1959 and were later
dancers at the Peppermint Lounge
(1). They had recorded
unsuccessfully for Colpix before
Spector signed them in 1963. That
year he produced their "Be My
Baby," "Baby, I Love You" and, in
1964, "(The Best Part of) Breakin'
Up" and "Walking in the Rain."
Possessive of Ronnie (4) (whom he
married in 1967), Spector nixed
plans for the trio to open for the
Beatles on their first U.S. tour. The
group later disbanded; Ronnie
divorced Spector in 1974. Her solo
releases include the Spector–George
Harrison-produced "Try Some, Buy
Some" (1971) and "Say Goodbye to
Hollywood" (1977) with the E Street
Band.

1

2

3

He's a Rebel

Darlene Love (Wright)(1) was a
member of the Blossoms before she
became lead vocalist for other
groups. Love's solo hits were
"(Today I Met) the Boy I'm Gonna
Marry" and "Wait 'til My Bobby Gets
Home" (1963). She recorded "He's a
Rebel" and "He's Sure the Boy I
Love" (1962) with the Crystals and
"Zip-A-Dee Doo-Dah" with Bob B.
Soxx and the Blue Jeans (2, Love,
middle). The Crystals (3) had hits
without Darlene: "Uptown," "Da
Doo Ron Ron" and "Then He Kissed
Me" (1962-63). The Righteous
Brothers (4), Bill Medley (left) and
Bobby Hatfield (right), epitomized
blue-eyed soul with "You've Lost
That Lovin' Feelin'," "Unchained
Melody" and "(You're My) Soul and
Inspiration" (1965-66). The age of
the Wall of Sound ended in 1966,
after Ike and Tina Turner's
Spector-produced "River Deep,
Mountain High" hit in England but
flopped at home. Spector (5, with Ike
and Tina) went into seclusion for
two years.

～ *River Deep*

Ike Turner first met Annie Mae Bullock in 1956, when she sat in with Turner and His Kings of Rhythm band one night. In 1958, they were married, and Ike rechristened his wife Tina. Tina had had no professional performing experience, but Ike had long been familiar in and around Memphis, where he worked as a bandleader, talent scout, guitarist and producer (B. B. King, Johnny Ace, Howlin' Wolf). The protorock classic "Rocket 88," credited to Jackie Brenston, was recorded with Ike's band. In 1960, Ike and Tina had their first hit with "A Fool in Love," followed by "It's Gonna Work Out Fine" and "I Idolize You" (1961). They revamped and emerged with the Ike and Tina Turner Revue, with nine musicians and three scantily clad female backup singers, the Ikettes. Tina's intense sexuality and blues-inspired vocals made the Revue a major draw. Their hits included "Come Together," "I Want to Take You Higher" (1970), "Proud Mary" (1971) and "Nutbush City Limits" (1973). Longtime favorites of the Rolling Stones, Ike and Tina opened the group's 1969 American tour. They divorced in 1976.

1

2

4

3

5

6

◄ *Sounds of Silence*

The folk revival began in the late '50s and reached a commercial peak in the early '60s with groups like the New Christy Minstrels (3). Formed by Randy Sparks in 1961, the Minstrels had three hits—"Green Green," "Saturday Night" (1963) and "Today" (1964). At one time or another, the group included Kenny Rogers, Kim Carnes, Mike Settle, John Denver, Gene Clark, Barry McGuire and Karen Black. (Carnes is in the middle on the left, Rogers at extreme right, Settle on left.) Carly and Lucy Simon (4), billed as the Simon Sisters, had a minor hit with "Winken, Blinken and Nod" in 1964 before they split up. Carly (left) emerged again as a singer/ songwriter with "That's the Way I've Always Heard It Should Be" in 1971. The Croces, Jim and his wife Ingrid (1), recorded *Approaching Day* in 1969. Three years later, Jim's solo career took off with "Operator" and "Bad, Bad Leroy Brown." Jim, Jake (Holmes) and Joan (Rivers) (2) were a folk-comedy trio popular in Greenwich Village.

4

3

1

2

3

4

5

6

🎵 *Sounds of Silence*

From prophetic to pathetic, Bob
Dylan (1, 2, 4, 7) was one of the finest
poets in pop music. With his style
encompassing folk, rock and
country, Dylan was the songwriter of
his generation and perhaps the
greatest single influence in '60s
rock. Robert Zimmerman legally
changed his name to Dylan in
August 1962, nineteen months after
moving to New York City. Within two
years, he was recording and playing
countless concerts, soon singing
with Joan Baez (5); they were
considered the King and Queen of
the folk movement. Dylan is seen
here in rare good humor with Sonny
and Cher (6). In the late '70s, Dylan
became born again, but his career
didn't. As a topical songwriter, Phil
Ochs's (3) success was second only
to Dylan's. Ochs sang at numerous
political events and wrote and
recorded "There But for Fortune,"
"I Ain't Marchin' Anymore" and
"Crucifixion."

7

4

5

🎵 *Sounds of Silence*

Paul Simon and Art Garfunkel met in the sixth grade. As Tom (Graph) and Jerry (Landis) (3), they had a minor 1957 hit, "Hey, Schoolgirl." They broke up, and Simon joined Tico and the Triumphs (1, Simon, middle) while Garfunkel, as Artie Garr (2), pursued a solo career. They met again in 1962, and two years later were signed to Columbia Records, which released "The Sounds of Silence." Simon and Garfunkel (5) became the most successful duo in pop with "Homeward Bound," "Mrs. Robinson" and the classic "Bridge over Troubled Water." They broke up in 1970. Janis Ian (4) was fifteen when her song about interracial love, "Society's Child," became a cause célèbre in 1967. She retired in 1972, but returned in 1975 with "At Seventeen." Blind singer/guitarist José Feliciano's (7) biggest hit was 1968's "Light My Fire." Canadian Gordon Lightfoot's (6) hits include "If You Could Read My Mind" and "Sundown."

6

7

1

2

♪ Boots of Spanish Leather

Ritchie Valens (3) (born Valenzuela) was *the* Chicano rocker, with "Come On, Let's Go" and "Donna" / "La Bamba" (1958-59). He died in the plane crash that also killed Buddy Holly in February 1959. Valens was one of Chris Montez's idols. Montez's (5) first hit, "Let's Dance" (1962), was his only rocker. Later hits, such as 1966's "Call Me," were pure croon. Cannibal and the Headhunters (4) inadvertently rewrote Chris Kenner's "Land of 1000 Dances," when Cannibal (Frankie Garcia) "na-na-na-na-na"-ed through some lyrics he'd forgotten. Sam the Sham (Domingo Samudio) and the Pharaohs (6) were an early Tex-Mex band, whose hits included "Wooly Bully," "JuJu Hand" and the lascivious "Li'l Red Riding Hood" (1965-66). Flint, Michigan's Question Mark and the Mysterians (2) recorded the Number One hit "96 Tears," which featured the Farfisa organ. Freddy Fender (1) had been a cult artist for nearly two decades when he hit with "Before the Next Teardrop Falls" and "Wasted Days and Wasted Nights" in 1975.

3

4

5

6

1

2

Goin' to Chicago

The Ice Man, Jerry Butler (4), recorded 1958's "For Your Precious Love" with the Impressions before beginning a solo career that would include such hits as "He Will Break Your Heart," "Moon River" and "Only the Strong Survive." In 1964, he recorded "Let It Be Me" and "Smile" with Betty Everett (5), who on her own recorded "You're No Good" (1963) and "The Shoop Shoop Song (It's in His Kiss)" (1964). Gene Chandler (2) was the lead singer on the Dukays' (1, Chandler, top) "The Girl's a Devil" (1961) and "Nite Owl" (1962.) He made his solo debut in 1962 with the million-selling classic "Duke of Earl." Dee Clark's (6) biggest hits were "Just Keep It Up," "Hey Little Girl" and "Raindrops" (1959-61). The Staple Singers (3) were formed in 1953 and soon began recording for Vee-Jay Records in the mid-'50s. They had their greatest success years later with "Respect Yourself" (1971) and a pair of Number Ones, "I'll Take You There" (1972) and "Let's Do It Again" (1975) on Stax.

3

4

6

5

✒ *Goin' to Chicago*

The '60s sound of Chicago was smooth and soulful. The Impressions (4), with lead singer Curtis Mayfield (middle), had numerous hits, including "Gypsy Woman," "It's All Right," "I'm So Proud," "Keep On Pushing," "Amen," "People Get Ready" and "We're a Winner" (1961-68). In 1970, Mayfield left for a solo career that yielded a million-selling LP, the *Superfly* soundtrack, and two gold singles, "Superfly" and "Freddie's Dead" (1972). Major Lance (1, with fans; 3) sang gospel in the '50s. His "The Monkey Time" (1963) and "Um, Um, Um, Um, Um, Um" (1964) were written and produced by Mayfield. Walter Jackson's (5) singles included "It's All Over" (1964) and "It's an Uphill Climb to the Bottom" (1966). Tyrone Davis's (2) career began in Mississippi where he performed as Tyrone the Wonder Boy. After moving to Chicago, he released several ballads, such as "Can I Change My Mind" (1968) and "Turn Back the Hands of Time" (1970).

✌ *Two Divided by Love*

In the early '60s, various types of duos came to the fore. Dick (St. John) and Deedee (Sperling) (1) recorded "The Mountain's High" in 1961, while attending high school. Other hits were "Young and in Love," "Turn Around" and "Thou Shalt Not Steal." Paul (Ray Hildebrand) and Paula (Jill Jackson) (3) went to Number One with "Hey Paula" in 1963, followed by "Young Lovers" and "First Quarrel." Brother and sister Nino Tempo and April Stevens's (2) Number One was "Deep Purple" (1963) and was followed by "Whispering" and "Stardust" (1963-64). Tempo was a sax player on many Phil Spector records. Don and Juan (Roland Trone and Claude Johnson of the Genies) (4) hit with "What's Your Name" (1962), and Tom (Eddie Thomas) and Jerrio (Jerry Murray) (6) hit in 1965 with "Boo-Ga-Loo." Also here: the legendary Foster Twins (5) and the Sims Twins (7), whose 1961 hit, "Soothe Me," was produced by Sam Cooke.

♫ *Two Divided by Love*

Peaches and Herb first hit in 1967, when Herb Fame and Francine Barker (1), who had been together for a few years, released "Close Your Eyes." Their later hits included "Love Is Strange" and "United" (1967-68) before Barker was replaced by Marlene Mack in 1968. Barker returned in 1969, but the duo soon split up. Herb then found his third Peaches, Linda Greene, and their "Shake Your Groove Thing" (1978) and "Reunited" (1979) outcharted and outsold the duo in its first two incarnations. Inez Foxx and her younger brother Charlie (4) recorded the 1963 classic "Mockingbird" (later revived by Carly Simon and James Taylor). Billy Vera and Judy Clay (5) (Dionne Warwick's cousin) had two modest hits: "Storybook Children" (1967) and "Country Girl—City Man" (1968). Billy now leads Billy and the Beaters, a Los Angeles soul band. Peggy Scott and Jo Jo Benson (2) met in 1968. He had formerly sung with Chuck Willis and the Blue Notes. Their hits were that year's "Lover's Holiday" and "Pickin' Wild Mountain Berries." Don Gardner and Dee Dee Ford's (3) best-known record was 1962's "I Need Your Loving."

4

5

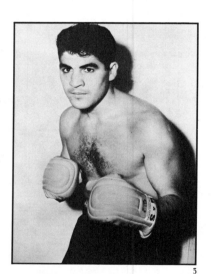

◖ *Jackie Wilson Said*

Detroit natives Jackie Wilson (5) and Marv Johnson (4) both launched their careers with the help of Motown founder Berry Gordy, Jr. Wilson, who was born in 1934, had been a Golden Gloves champ (3). He met Gordy in 1957, four years after leaving Billy Ward's Dominoes (2, Wilson on right). Gordy wrote Wilson's first two hits, "Reet Petite" and "To Be Loved." "Lonely Teardrops," "Baby Workout" and "(Your Love Keeps Lifting Me) Higher and Higher" followed, but none could capture the wild sexual frenzy Wilson's live shows inspired. In 1957, Gordy found Johnson, for whom he wrote "Come to Me" and "You Got What It Takes." Wilson's later career was mostly limited to the nostalgia circuit. In September 1975, he suffered a heart attack while performing at a Dick Clark (1, earlier) oldies show in Cherry Hill, New Jersey. He languished in a coma until his death on January 21, 1984.

5

221

♪ *Dancing in the Street*

The fledgling Motown empire got its
start when Barrett Strong (4)
recorded "Money" for Gordy's Anna
label; it was Strong's only hit, though
he later wrote and produced "Papa
Was a Rollin' Stone" and "I Wish It
Would Rain." Brian Holland, Lamont
Dozier and Eddie Holland (6),
Motown's premier producers and
songwriters, were responsible for
more Top Ten hits than any team in
history. Tenor sax player Jr. Walker
(Autry DeWalt Walker, Jr.) (7, top
left) and the All Stars recorded
"Shotgun" (1965) and "What Does It
Take (to Win Your Love)" (1969).
Jimmy Ruffin's (3) biggest hit was
1966's "What Becomes of the
Brokenhearted." His brother, David
Ruffin (2), who left the Temptations
in 1968, hit with "My Whole World
Ended" (1969) and "Walk Away from
Love" (1975). Bobby Taylor and the
Vancouvers (5), featuring Tommy
Chong of Cheech and Chong fame
(left), had a hit in 1968 with "Does
Your Mama Know about Me." Also:
an Apollo Theatre marquee
announcing a Motown bill (1).

5

7

6

✒ *Dancing in the Street*

Gladys Knight was just eight years
(1) old when she won the grand
prize on *Ted Mack's Original
Amateur Hour*. She went
professional with the Pips (2), which
included her brother Merald and
cousin William Guest; cousin
Edward Patten joined later. Their
first hit was Johnny Otis's "With
Every Beat of My Heart" in 1961,
followed by "Letter Full of Tears."
Once signed to Motown, their streak
picked up in 1967 with "I Heard It
through the Grapevine," "If I Were
Your Woman" (1970) and "Neither
One of Us" (1973). Their second hit
on Buddah was also their first
Number One, 1973's "Midnight Train
to Georgia." The Isley Brothers (4, 5)
—Ronald, Rudolph and O'Kelly—hit
with "Shout" in 1958. Later hits
included "This Old Heart of Mine,"
"That Lady" and "Fight the Power"
(1962-75). The Velvelettes (3) had a
minor hit with "Needle in a
Haystack" in 1964. Their other claim
to fame is having recorded the
original version of Bananarama's
1982 club hit "He Was Really Sayin'
Somethin'" in 1965.

1

2

5

3

4

1

🎵 *Dancing in the Street*

Had Smokey Robinson only led the Miracles, his place in history would be assured. But Robinson, whom Bob Dylan once called "America's greatest living poet," was also a prolific songwriter whose compositions provided hits for virtually every Motown act. Robinson, who had formed the Miracles in high school, met Berry Gordy when he was seventeen. Gordy and Robinson became friends. A year later, the Miracles— Robinson, Ronnie White, Pete Moore and Bobby Rogers—recorded "Got a Job," an answer record to the Silhouettes' "Get a Job." In 1960, "Shop Around" became Motown's first R&B Number One. The Miracles went on to chart twenty-six more Top Forty hits ("More Love," "The Tracks of My Tears," "Ooo Baby Baby") before Robinson left to assume a vice-presidency and a solo career at Motown in 1972. Here, pictured with an early Miracle, his wife Claudette (1) and with Ed Sullivan (4).

2

3

4

5

♪ *Dancing in the Street*

Marvin Gaye (3, 4) had been singing since the age of three. When Gaye was nineteen, Harvey Fuqua brought him into a latter-day version of the Moonglows, with whom he was appearing when Berry Gordy discovered him. Signed to Motown in 1961, Gaye was a session drummer before his 1962 hit, "Stubborn Kind of Fellow." In addition to his solo hits—"I'll Be Doggone," "Hitch Hike," "How Sweet It Is to Be Loved by You"— Gaye also recorded a series of hit duets with Mary Wells ("Once upon a Time," "What's the Matter with You") and Kim Weston ("It Takes Two"). But his most celebrated duets were with Tammi Terrell (5)—"Ain't No Mountain High Enough," "Ain't Nothing like the Real Thing." After Terrell collapsed in his arms onstage in 1967, Gaye avoided live performances. She died of a brain tumor three years later. Gaye's later records, such as *What's Going On* (1971), were more introspective. Here, Gaye's live backup singers, the Marvelettes (1, 2).

3

4

5

1

2

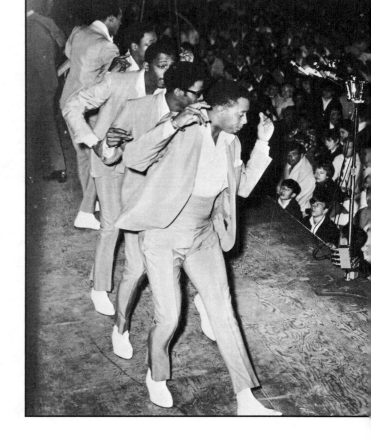

3

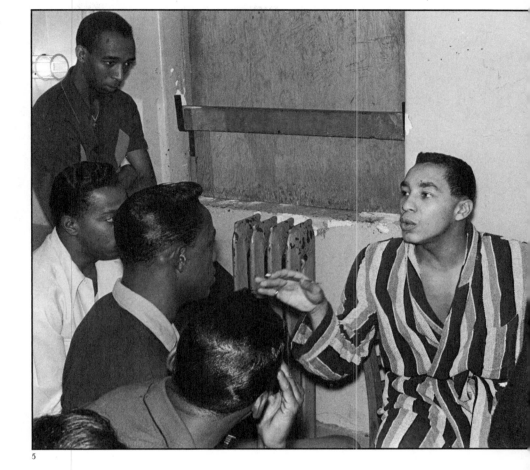

5

4

🎵 *Dancing in the Street*

The Temptations' roots go back to
Detroit in the late '50s, where the
group—Eddie Kendricks, Paul
Williams, Otis Williams, Eldridge
Bryant and Melvin Franklin—
formed the Primes (3). Signed to
Motown in 1960, the Primes
recorded with minimal success until
1963, when David Ruffin replaced
Bryant and Smokey Robinson
produced their version of his "The
Way You Do the Things You Do" in
1964. Now the Temptations (1, 2, 4),
they hit a winning streak, producing
more than two dozen Top Twenty
hits and becoming the most
successful black male vocal group of
the decade. The next year, "My Girl"
(which composer Smokey taught
them backstage at the Apollo, 5) hit
Number One, as would "I Can't Get
Next to You" (1969), "Just My
Imagination" (1971) and "Papa Was
a Rollin' Stone" (1972). Ruffin left in
1967 for a solo career, as did Eddie
Kendricks and Paul Williams four
years later. Williams died in 1973.

3

4

5

✒ *Dancing in the Street*

The original Supremes—Diana Ross,
Florence Ballard and Mary Wilson—
were the most important and
successful girl group of the '60s.
Founded in Detroit in the late '50s,
they recorded ten sides before they
topped the chart in 1964 with
"Where Did Our Love Go." Their
twelve Number Ones were "Where
Did Our Love Go," "Baby Love,"
"Come See about Me," "Stop! In the
Name of Love," "Back in My Arms
Again," "I Hear a Symphony," "You
Can't Hurry Love," "You Keep Me
Hangin' On," "Love Is Here and Now
You're Gone," "The Happening,"
"Love Child" and their last hit with
Ross, "Someday We'll Be Together"
(1964-69). The Supremes performed
with the Temptations on Ed
Sullivan's show (6, Ross with David
Ruffin), which led to an hour-long
special *T.C.B.*

6

1

2

3

♫ *Dancing in the Street*

The Contours (2) signed to Motown after Jackie Wilson introduced their lead singer—and his cousin—Hubert Johnson to Berry Gordy. The group's hits included "Do You Love Me" (1962) and "First I Look at the Purse" (1965). Mary Wells (3) was Motown's first female star. By the time she was eighteen years of age, she had charted three Top Ten hits, "The One Who Really Loves You," "You Beat Me to the Punch" and "Two Lovers" (1962). Her biggest hit was the 1964 Number One, "My Guy." That year she recorded two duets with Marvin Gaye, "What's the Matter with You Baby" and "Once upon a Time." Martha (Reeves) and the Vandellas (4, 5) were the label's gutsiest girl group, with such hits as "Come and Get These Memories,"

"Heat Wave," "Quicksand," "Dancing in the Streets," "Nowhere to Run," "I'm Ready for Love" and "Jimmy Mack" (1963-67). The Spinners (1), with lead singer Harvey Fuqua (formerly of the Moonglows), charted with "That's What Girls Are Made For" in 1961. They joined Motown in 1965, but didn't really break big until the '70s with "It's a Shame" and "I'll Be Around."

3

4

♪ *Dancing in the Street*

Steveland ⌐ ⌐kins was born blind, but by the time Miracle Ronnie White introduced him to Berry Gordy, at age ten, Stevie could sing, and play harmonica, drums and keyboards. Gordy renamed him Little Stevie Wonder, and, in 1963, when he was just thirteen, he scored his first Number One hit, "Fingertips (Pt. 2)." Other hits included "Uptight (Everything's Alright)" (1966), "I Was Made to Love Her" (1967), "For Once in My Life" (1968) and "Signed, Sealed, Delivered, I'm Yours" (1970). In 1971, he became the first Motown artist to be given complete artistic control. His later hits—"Superstition" (1971), "Living for the City" (1972) and "Do I Do" (1982)—further solidified his standing as one of the most accomplished and popular black entertainers of all time. Wonder is pictured here with Cassius Clay (1) and Jackie Wilson (5).

5

1

2

〰 *Wipe Out*

Dick Dale's guitar style—a heavily reverbed twang—was one of the most influential in '60s rock & roll, later evident in the music of the Beach Boys, among others. With his Del-Tones, Dale scored two instrumental surf rock hits, "Let's Go Trippin'" (1961) and "Misirlou" (1962), that kicked off the surf-music craze. In fact, the Beach Boys covered both of these hits on early albums. The King of Surf Guitar returned in 1963 with "The Scavenger." Dale is pictured here with Annette (3), and promoting his movie, *Beach Party* (1), he is with promo man Al Courey (third from left), who later ran RSO Records and was responsible for *Saturday Night Fever* soundtrack. In addition to his prowess on the guitar, Dale also played other instruments. Here (2) he is on trumpet.

3

4

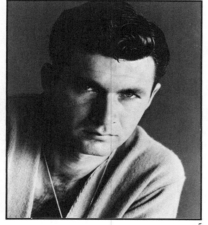

5

∿ *Wipe Out*

The Beach Boys—brothers Brian,
Dennis and Carl Wilson, cousin
Mike Love and Al Jardine—were the
only American band that both
challenged and inspired the Beatles.
Through Brian's songs, the Beach
Boys celebrated—and seemed to
invent—a mythic American youth of
hot cars, California girls, sun,
freedom and surf. Within months of
their 1962 debut, "Surfin'," the
Beach Boys had the first of dozens of
hits, "Surfin' Safari." Their three
Number Ones were "I Get Around"
(1964), "Help Me Rhonda" (1965)
and Brian's production masterpiece,
"Good Vibrations" (1966). In 1967,
Brian (2) suffered a series of
nervous breakdowns. The group
continued recording and touring,
with Bruce Johnston replacing Brian
on the road (1, with both Johnston
and Brian). Ironically, only Dennis,
who suggested the idea for "Surfin'"
and who drowned on December 28,
1983, in the harbor at Marina del
Rey, had ever surfed. Several days
later he was buried at sea.

3

4

6

5

〰 *Wipe Out*

The real Rip Chords were future Beach Boy Bruce Johnston, producer Terry Melcher and some studio musicians, but the trio here (5) is the touring group. The Rip Chords' hits were "Hey Little Cobra" and "Three Window Coupe" (1964). The Hondells (1) were another studio aggregation who went Top Ten in 1964 with "Little Honda." The record was produced by Mike Curb and Nik Venet when, according to Venet, Capitol Records wouldn't let the Beach Boys record the song. Brian Wilson gave them the song and helped out on the session. The Surfaris' (2) first hit, 1963's "Wipe Out," is distinguished by the maniacal opening laugh and what is now probably the best-known drum solo in rock. Their followup that year was "Surfer Joe." The Duals (4) released one record, "Stick Shift" (1961), and the Astronauts (3) recorded a number of albums in the early '60s, but their only chart record was "Baja" in 1963.

1

2

3

4

〜 *Wipe Out*

Jan Berry and Dean Torrence were the top surf duo, with over a dozen hits in less than eight years. The two met in junior high school. With Arnie Ginsberg (1, left) they recorded "Jennie Lee" in 1958. By the next year, Jan and Dean (2, 3, 5) released "Baby Talk," followed in 1963 by a tune Brian Wilson cowrote, "Surf City." Despite a slew of surf hits—"Dead Man's Curve," "Little Old Lady (from Pasadena)" and "Drag City"—their relationship was showing signs of strain by 1966, when Jan ran his Corvette into a parked truck and sustained brain damage from which he has yet to fully recover. In the early days, the Beach Boys and Jan and Dean frequently sang on each other's records: Dean sings lead on the Beach Boys' "Barbara Ann." Jan is pictured here in the studio with producer Bones Howe (4, left).

5

1

2

❧ *Wipe Out*

Although they were big West Coast concert acts, most surf bands did not cut hit singles. The Rumblers (2) barely squeaked onto the charts with "Boss" in 1963; Jim Messina made it only after leaving the Jesters (3, Messina at right) and teaming up with Kenny Loggins; and the Crossfires' (1) label made them change their name to the Turtles. Jerry Kole and the Challengers (4) never charted. The Ventures (6), however, led by guitarists Don Wilson and Bob Bogle, had several hits, including "Walk, Don't Run," "Ghost Riders in the Sky," "Perfidia," "Lullaby of the Leaves" and "Diamond Head" (1960-65). In 1969 they charted with "Hawaii Five-O." The Marketts' (5) "Out of Limits" was a surf-ized version of the *Outer Limits* TV-show theme. Their next biggest hit was another tube tune, "Batman's Theme" (1966).

3

4

5

6

4

5

✺ *Soul Stew*

Pianist Martin Denny (4) had a Top
Ten hit in 1959 with "Quiet Village."
Two years later, saxophonist Eddie
Harris (2) made the Top Forty with
"Exodus." In 1962, organist Jimmy
Smith (6, Smith, left) "Walk on the
Wild Side—Part I" was a major hit.
Guitarist Wes Montgomery's (1) 1967
instrumental version of the
Association's "Windy" also charted.
Montgomery died the next year.
Saxman King Curtis (Curtis Ousley)
(3) was a major session player. He
performed on the Coasters' "Yakety
Yak" in 1957. He also led the
Kingpins, a soul band that backed
Aretha Franklin, among others.
Curtis died on August 13, 1971, at age
thirty-seven, after being stabbed
while trying to stop a street fight.
Billy Preston (5) played keyboards
for the Beatles before returning to a
solo career that yielded "Outa
Space" (1972), "Will It Go 'round in
Circles" (1973) and "Nothing from
Nothing" (1974).

6

3

4

5

6

❧ *Tossin' and Turnin'*

When Gary Anderson's (1, 2) producer credited his first single to Gary "U.S." Bonds, Anderson was surprised, but the name stuck. Bonds's five Top Ten hits were "New Orleans," "Quarter to Three," "School Is Out," "Dear Lady Twist" and "Twist Twist Señora" (1960-62). His 1981 comeback LP was produced by Bruce Springsteen. In 1960, Jimmy Jones (4) had a pair of Top Tens: "Handy Man" (later recorded by James Taylor) and "Good Timin'." That year, Nat Kendrick (5) and the Swans released "(Do the) Mashed Potatoes (Part 1)." Bobby Lewis (3) had the Number One song of 1961, "Tossin' and Turnin'," and hit again the next year with "One Track Mind." Slim Harpo (6) (James Moore) had but two hits, "Rainin' in My Heart" (1961) and "Baby Scratch My Back" (1966), but his guitar, harmonica and vocal styles were influential. He died in 1970 at age forty-six.

1

2   3   4

254

5

6

♪~ *Tossin' and Turnin'*

Ron Holden (6, right, with Bob Keane, left, and *Shindig!* host Jimmy O'Neil) recorded the 1960 hit "Love You So" with Bruce Johnston. In 1961, Gene McDaniels (3) had two major hits, "A Hundred Pounds of Clay" and "Tower of Strength," followed in 1962 with "Chip Chip." In 1965, Mel Carter's (4) two biggest hits were "Hold Me, Thrill Me, Kiss Me" and "(All of a Sudden) My Heart Sings," and Jewel Akens (2) told us 'bout "The Birds and the Bees." Dobie Gray's (5, with fans) 1965 smash was "The 'In' Crowd," but it was eight years before his next big one, 1973's country-soul "Drift Away." Brenton Wood (1) (named for Brentwood, California) scored in 1967 with "The Oogum Boogum Song" and "Gimme Little Sign."

1

2

3

4

∼ *Tossin' and Turnin'*

Billy Stewart (5) sang with the
Rainbows before embarking on a
solo career. His hits were "I Do Love
You," "Sitting in the Park" (1965) and
a soulful version of George
Gershwin's "Summertime" (1966).
Stewart was killed in a car crash in
1970. In the '50s, Jimmy (Castor) (1)
and the Juniors recorded "I Promise
to Remember," which Frankie
Lymon and the Teenagers covered
with greater success. Interestingly,
Castor occasionally subbed for
Lymon on tours. He also played sax
on Dave "Baby" Cortez's "Rinky
Dink." Castor came back with his
Bunch in 1966 with "Hey, Leroy, Your
Mama's Callin' You" and six years
later with "Troglodyte (Cave Man)."
J. J. Jackson (2) had a 1966 hit, "But
It's All Right." Two artists of the era
had dance hits: the Fantastic Johnny
C (Corley) (4) released "Boogaloo
down Broadway" (1967) and Cliff
Nobles (3) & Co. did "The Horse"
(1968).

5

🎵 *Tossin' and Turnin'*

Little Eva (6) (Narcissus Boyd) was baby-sitting for Carole King's children when King asked her to record "The Loco-Motion" with the Cookies. The song inspired the dance craze and hit Number One in 1962. Eva's other hits were "Keep Your Hands off My Baby" and "Swingin' on a Star," with Big Dee Irwin. After Claudine Clark (4) recorded "Party Lights" (1962) in a Chancellor Records office, superstition dictated that an LP should be cut there as well. It bombed. Fontella Bass's (3) memorable 1965 hit was "Rescue Me." In 1960, Damita Jo (2) recorded "I'll Save the Last Dance for You," an answer record to the Drifters hit "Save the Last Dance for Me." Ketty Lester (1), who'd toured with Cab Calloway, hit with 1962's "Love Letters." The same year, singer/guitarist Barbara Lynn (5) (Ozone) recorded her "You'll Lose a Good Thing."

1

2

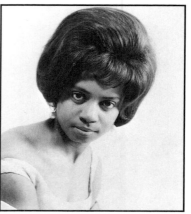

3

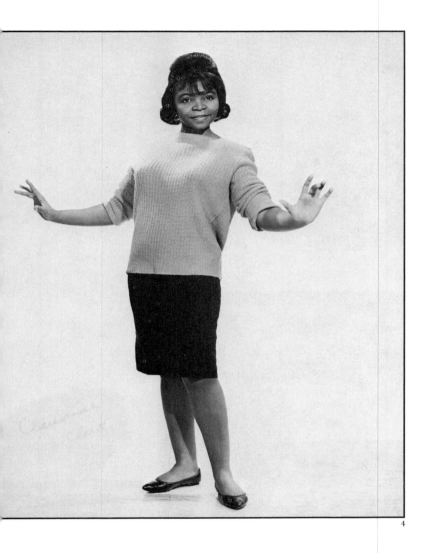

5

6

1

2

3

◈ *Tossin' and Turnin'*

Billy Bland (6) (no relation to Bobby Bland) had a Top Ten hit in 1960 with "Let the Little Girl Dance." The next year, Chuck Jackson (3), who had sung with the Dell-Vikings from 1957 to 1959, had his first of two hits, "I Don't Want to Cry," followed by Burt Bacharach's "Any Day Now." Jimmy Soul (1) (James McCleese) first hit in 1962 with "Twistin' Matilda." The rock calypso followup was the 1963 Number One, "If You Wanna Be Happy." Songwriter Freddie Scott (5), who'd penned Paul Anka's "It Only Lasts for a Little While," had two hits of his own, "Hey Girl" (1963) and "Are You Lonely for Me" (1967). Sam Cooke produced Johnnie Morisette's (4) "Meet Me at the Twistin' Place" in 1962, the same year that Johnny Thunder (2) recorded "Loop De Loop."

1

✺ *Tossin' and Turnin'*

Within a year of signing to Chess
Records, Etta James (1) released the
first of a string of R&B hits that
would include "All I Could Do Was
Cry," "Trust in Me," "Stop the
Wedding" and "Tell Mama"
(1960-67). In 1962, "Little" Esther
Phillips (2), who had retired in 1954,
returned with the country-soul
"Release Me," produced by Kenny
Rogers's brother Lelan. She
continued to record and had a disco
hit in 1975 with "What a Difference a
Day Makes." Detroit singer Barbara
Lewis's (7) biggest hits were "Hello
Stranger" (1963) and "Baby I'm
Yours" (1965). Jan Bradley's (6) only
Top Twenty hit was 1963's "Mama
Didn't Lie." Among the few who
wrote the songs they recorded were
ex-beauty queen Maxine Brown (3)
("All in My Mind" and "Funny,"
1961) and Barbara Mason (5) ("Yes,
I'm Ready," 1965). Doris Troy (4) is
best remembered for "Just One
Look" (1963); she later recorded
for Apple.

2

3

~ *California Dreamin'*

Though it was San Francisco's '60s music-cultural scene that captured national media attention, L.A.'s folk rockers ultimately proved more influential. The scene's principal character was Dylanesque songwriter Philip (P. F.) Sloan (4), whose most memorable composition was the Number One hit for Barry McGuire (5, left with Sloan), "Eve of Destruction." Sloan often worked with Steve Barri (3, left), who wrote for the Grass Roots and the Turtles. Sloan-Barri recorded "Where Were You When I Needed You" as the Grass Roots (2), but then bestowed their "group" name on the 13th Floor. The new Grass Roots had thirteen Top Forty hits. The most successful L.A. folk-rock outfit was the Association (1). Their predominantly ballady hits featured intricate multivoice harmonies. "Cherish" and "Windy" both went Number One.

4

5

6

〜 *California Dreamin'*

New York City-born Johnny Rivers
(5; 6, third from left) eventually
became one of L.A.'s most prolific
hitmakers. Rivers's first hit was a
revived "Memphis," one of his
thirteen Top Twenty singles
between 1964 and 1977, and he was
one of the few white singers to
record credible versions of current
Motown hits ("Baby I Need Your
Lovin'," "The Tracks of My Tears").
Rivers's producer, Lou Adler, also
discovered and produced the
Mamas and the Papas (2, 3), headed
by John Phillips, an ex-Journeyman
along with Scott McKenzie (1,
Phillips, left; McKenzie, front). With
Denny Doherty, Mama Cass Elliot
and his wife Michelle, Phillips
recorded his "California Dreamin'"
and "Monday, Monday." "California
Dreamin'" was originally intended
for and recorded by Barry McGuire;
producer Adler merely put the
Mamas and the Papas' voices in
place of McGuire's and replaced the
harmonica solo with a flute. Here (4),
Lou Adler (right) is pictured with
Bobby Roberts (left) and Johnny
Rivers (middle).

1

2

3

4

❧ *California Dreamin'*

L.A.'s Fifth Dimension, originally envisaged as a black Mamas and the Papas, created a slick blend of pop soul. Discovered by Johnny Rivers, produced by Bones Howe, and with songs by then-little-known Jimmy Webb, the Fifth Dimension produced six gold singles, including "Up, Up and Away" (4, with Howe, second right, and Webb, right). Enjoying less national popularity were such area acts as the Lewis and Clarke Expedition (3)—Travis Lewis being Michael Murphey (middle) and Boomer Clarke being Boomer Castleman (right). Each had a 1975 hit: Murphey's "Wildfire" and Castleman's "Judy Mae." The Chad Mitchell Trio, who recorded the novelty hit "Lizzie Borden," soon became the Mitchell Trio (1) when John Denver (middle) replaced Chad. The obscure Steeltown Two (2) (brothers Carson and Van Dyke Parks) was comprised of two songwriters. Van Dyke Parks later released some eclectic LPs and cowrote several songs with Beach Boy Brian Wilson ("Surf's Up," "Heroes and Villains").

1

✒ *California Dreamin'*

In 1965, the Byrds returned self-respect to American rock & roll, which had taken a back seat to the British Invasion. Though the Byrds' hits ended by 1967, their sound—Roger McGuinn's twelve-string guitar and the uplifting, seamless harmonies of David Crosby, Gene Clark and Chris Hillman—can be heard today in the records of Tom Petty, among others. Crosby came from Les Baxter's Balladeers (2, Crosby, bottom, left), and Clark from the New Christy Minstrels. Crosby (3, right, with McGuinn) left in 1967. McGuinn (5) led the Byrds through several incarnations until 1973. In 1968, their *Sweetheart of the Rodeo* heralded the coming age of country rock; Gram Parsons, a Byrd for that one LP, left to form the Flying Burrito Brothers in 1969.

2

3

4

5

1

2

3

4

♫ *California Dreamin'*

The Buffalo Springfield (2, 4) are best remembered for the acts they spawned rather than for the three albums' worth of music they released from 1966 to 1968. Their only pop hit was Stills's "For What It's Worth" (1967). When the band broke up, Steve Stills formed Crosby, Stills and Nash, Neil Young went solo, and Richie Furay and Jim Messina began Poco. The Turtles (5, 6) had the hits the Springfield couldn't. Though their hit singles were buoyant pop, singer/writers Howard Kaylan and Mark Volman also added an irreverent sense of humor. Among their Top Ten hits were "Happy Together," "She'd Rather Be with Me" (1967), "Elenore" (1968) and "You Showed Me" (1969). Turtles Jim Pons and John Barbata were in the Leaves (1), who had the U.S. hit version of "Hey Joe." The Rising Sons (3) included Ry Cooder (right) and Taj Mahal (left).

1

3

2

4

🎵 *Shake a Tail Feather*

The Five Du-Tones' (5) memorable hit was 1963's "Shake a Tail Feather." The following year, the Larks (3) (who had been known as Don Julian and the Meadowlarks) hit with "The Jerk." In 1966, Detroit's Capitols (4) cashed in on the dance craze with "Cool Jerk." Dyke (Lester Christian) and the Blazers (2) cut "Funky Broadway" in 1967; a few years later, Dyke was shot to death during a show on Broadway. Jay (Proctor) and the Techniques' (1) two 1967 hits— "Apples, Peaches, Pumpkin Pie" and "Keep the Ball Rollin'"—were inspired by kids' games, while Archie Bell and the Drells (6) (from Houston, Texas) made the great dance records "Tighten Up" and "I Can't Stop Dancing" in 1968.

5

6

∿ *Shake a Tail Feather*

Bobby Womack and his brothers began singing gospel as the Womack Brothers. They were discovered by Sam Cooke, who produced their pop releases as the Valentinos (2): "Lookin' for a Love" (1962) and "It's All Over Now" (1964). George Clinton (1) founded the Parliaments (3) in 1955. Originally a doo-wop group, the Parliaments ventured into soul rock with "(I Wanna) Testify" in 1967, and scored in the '70s with a whole new thang—the Parliament/Funkadelic empire. Clinton, who counts Dr. Funkenstein and Maggot Overlord among his several *noms de disques*, says, "Free your ass and your mind will follow." Their popular songs include "One Nation under a Groove" (1978) and "(not just) Knee Deep—Part I" (1979). Also pictured: Bobby Moore (5), who with the Rhythm Aces did "Searching for My Love" (1966), the Marvelows (4) and Bobby Patterson and the Mustangs (6).

1

2

3

4

5

6

5   6

7

✺ *It's My Party*

Female singers in the early '60s could be coy, tough or both. For the most part, they were teens. Linda Scott (3) was sixteen when she had two 1961 Top Ten hits, "I've Told Every Little Star" and "Don't Bet Money Honey." The next year, eighteen-year-old Marci Blane (2) had her only hit, "Bobby's Girl," as did Sandy Stewart (5) with "My Coloring Book." In 1963, Little Peggy March's (4) "I Will Follow Him," which she recorded at age fifteen, went to Number One. Diane Renay's (1) 1964 singles had a nautical theme: "Navy Blue" and "Kiss Me, Sailor." By far the most consistent of the lot was Lesley Gore (6, 7). At sixteen, working with producer Quincy Jones, Gore recorded the teen-soap "It's My Party" and its vengeful followup, "Judy's Turn to Cry." Her other two 1963 hits were "She's a Fool" and the protofeminist "You Don't Own Me." Later hits included "That's the Way Boys Are," "Maybe I Know" (1964), "Sunshine, Lollipops and Rainbows" (1965) and "California Nights" (1967).

279

4

5

6

〜 *It's My Party*

Timi Yuro (1), the early '60s' premier white female soul singer, hit with "Hurt," "What's a Matter Baby" and "Make the World Go Away" (1961-63). Trini Lopez (5, with Dick Clark) jazzed up two Peter, Paul and Mary recordings—"If I Had a Hammer" (1963) and "Lemon Tree" (1965)—recorded them live at P.J.'s and made them danceable hits. Gale Garnett's (3) one hit was 1964's "We'll Sing in the Sunshine." Bobbie Gentry (2) (né Street) recorded 1967's "Ode to Billie Joe." Glen Campbell (6), had been a session guitarist for Phil Spector before his minor 1961 hit, "Turn Around, Look at Me." He worked as a session guitarist with other groups, including the Monkees. Campbell's greater success came with "Gentle on My Mind," "Wichita Lineman" and "Galveston" (1967-69). Leon Russell (4, lower right), is shown here at a studio session with Marvin Gaye and the Blossoms (with whom he was a regular on *Shindig!*). Russell wrote for and recorded with Joe Cocker before releasing his own hits, such as 1972's "Tight Rope."

✺ *It's My Party*

Bruce Channel's (4) 1962 Number
One "Hey! Baby" featured Delbert
McClinton on harmonica. Roy Head
(1) scored in 1965 with "Treat Her
Right." Ray Stevens's (7) hits
included not only his best-known
novelties—"Ahab the Arab" (whose
camel, Clyde, was named for
McPhatter) and "Gitarzan"—but
more serious fare like 1968's "Mr.
Businessman." Joe South's (3) hits
were "Games People Play" (1969)
and "Walk a Mile in My Shoes"
(1970). He wrote and produced Billy
Joe Royal's (5) "Down in the
Boondocks," "I Knew You When"
and "Hush" (1965-67). B. J. Thomas
(2, middle) had a series of Top Ten
hits: "I'm So Lonesome I Could Cry,"
"Hooked on a Feeling," "Raindrops
Keep Fallin' on My Head" and "I Just
Can't Help Believing" (1966-70).
Also pictured: Wayne Cochran (6),
the white James Brown.

1

2

4

3

5

6

7

4

5

6

♫ *It's My Party*

Jackie DeShannon (4) was known as
a songwriter (Brenda Lee's "Dum
Dum") before she came to
prominence as a performer with her
hit of Burt Bacharach's "What the
World Needs Now Is Love" (1965).
She cowrote the 1981 international
smash "Bette Davis Eyes." In the
mid-'60s, Jeff Barry produced Neil
Diamond's (3) "Solitary Man,"
"Cherry, Cherry," "Girl You'll Be a
Woman Soon" and "Sweet Caroline"
(1966-69), each of which sold
millions. Later, Barry produced
Andy Kim's (1) "Baby, I Love You"
(1969) and the 1974 Number One
"Rock Me Gently." Ron Dante (5)
sang lead on the Detergents' novelty,
"Leader of the Laundromat," and, in
the late '60s, was the voice of Archie
on the studio group's hits, such as
"Sugar Sugar." After the Righteous
Brothers split up, Bill Medley's (2)
solo career yielded two 1968 hits,
"Brown Eyed Woman" and "Peace,
Brother, Peace." Also here, future
Three Dog Night vocalist Danny
Hutton (6), circa his 1965 recording,
"Roses and Rainbows."

1

ᴥ *It's My Party*

Neither Nancy Sinatra, Merrilee
Rush nor Sissy Spacek saw their
popularity as singers transcend the
'60s. Spacek (1, middle), who
recorded in 1969 under the name
Rainbo, became a major actress. Her
portrayal of Loretta Lynn in *Coal
Miner's Daughter* and her country
singing were so convincing that she
released an LP of C&W in 1983.
Nancy Sinatra's (2) flat, nasal voice
was perfect for "These Boots Are
Made for Walking" (1966). She
duetted with her famous dad on
"Somethin' Stupid" and with Lee
Hazlewood on "Jackson" (1967), but
the hits stopped the next year.
Merrilee Rush (3) scored with
"Angel of the Morning" (1968). She
never had another hit. Linda
Ronstadt (5) became the preeminent
female singer of the mid-'70s and
early '80s. Here with the Stone
Poneys (4) who hit with "Different
Drum" (1968).

2

3

4

5

3

4

♪ *Soul Deep*

Furry Lewis may have been one of the first musicians to play bottleneck guitar. At any rate, in his nearly ninety years, he played with everyone from W. C. Handy to Lonnie Mack. He is pictured here (2, left) with his producer Don Nix, saxman for the Mar-Keys ("Last Night"). Ironing Board Sam (1) was one of several Memphis eccentrics. Sam, whose instrument was made from an ironing board, would play while standing atop a high wire— without a net. Bill Black had been Elvis Presley's bassist before he started his own Combo (3). Their hits included "Smokie, Part 2" (1959) and "Josephine" (1960). Black died following surgery for a brain tumor in 1965. The Box Tops (5) and the Gentrys (4) were the only major white groups to emerge from Memphis. In 1965, the Gentrys released "Keep On Dancing." The Box Tops, with lead singer Alex Chilton, had a string of hits—"The Letter," "Cry like a Baby" and "Soul Deep" (1967-69).

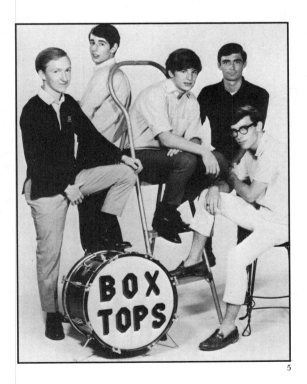

5

↝ *Soul Deep*

Booker T. Jones (1) joined Stax
Records as a session musician and,
with the MGs (for Memphis Group)
(2, 3), backed almost all of the Stax-
Volt roster and some of Atlantic's
soul artists. They got together in
1962 after Jones convinced Steve
Cropper (6) and Donald "Duck"
Dunn (5), then members of the Mar-
Keys—a group Jones had also been
in—to join his new band. Their 1962
hit was "Green Onions," which later
became popular with Britain's Mods.
Other hits included "Boot-Leg"
(1965), "My Sweet Potato" (1966),
"Hip Hug-Her" (1967), "Time Is
Tight" (1969), "Groovin'" and "Soul
Limbo" (1968). There were some
shifts in personnel, but the best-
known version of the MGs consisted
of bassist Dunn, drummer Al
Jackson (4) (dubbed the
Timekeeper for his superhuman
ability to keep perfect time) and
guitarist Steve Cropper, who also
cowrote "In the Midnight Hour"
(with Wilson Pickett), "Knock on
Wood" (with Eddie Floyd) and
"(Sittin' on) the Dock of the Bay"
(with Otis Redding). Jackson was
shot to death in Memphis in 1975.
Cropper and Dunn later played with
the Blues Brothers on their one and
only national tour.

2

4

5

6

291

1

2

3

4

⌁ *Soul Deep*

Rufus Thomas (5, 6) was a DJ at
WDIA in Memphis before he broke
big with a series of dance hits: "The
Dog," "Walking the Dog," "Can Your
Monkey Do the Dog," "Do the Funky
Chicken," "(Do the) Push and Pull"
and "The Breakdown" (1963-71). His
daughter Carla Thomas's (1) hits
included "Gee Whiz" (1961) and
"B-A-B-Y" (1966). Her debut was a
duet with her father, "Cause I Love
You" (1960). Isaac Hayes cowrote
"B-A-B-Y," "Hold On, I'm Comin'"
and other hits. His 1969 LP *Hot
Buttered Soul* went Top Ten, and his
"Theme from Shaft" went to
Number One. He is pictured here
with guitarist Albert King (2, left)
and songwriting partner David
Porter (4, right). William Bell's (3)
hits were "You Don't Miss Your
Water" (1962) and "I Forgot to Be
Your Lover" (1969).

5

6

1

2

3

4

5

6

✧ *Soul Deep*

In 1960, Satellite Records took over an old theater and transformed a storefront into a record store; the next year Satellite became Stax (1). In the fall of 1960, Rufus Thomas brought in Carla Thomas to record "Gee Whiz." Eddie Floyd (4) had founded the Falcons in 1956, but left them in 1962 for a solo career (Wilson Pickett took his place). His first hit, "Knock on Wood," came four years later. He also wrote songs for Pickett, Solomon Burke and Carla Thomas. Perhaps Stax's greatest successes were Sam (Moore) and Dave (Prater) (2, 5), who after several years together finally scored in 1966 with "You Don't Know like I Know" and "Hold On, I'm Coming"; "Soul Man" followed in 1967. Johnnie Taylor (3) began singing professionally for the Five Echoes in 1955; after replacing Sam Cooke in the Soul Stirrers, he went solo. His first big hit was 1968's "Who's Making Love." In 1976, he was awarded one of the first platinum singles for "Disco Lady." Mel (Harden) and Tim (McPherson) (6) had their biggest hits before signing to Stax. Their 1969 "Backfield in Motion" was produced by Gene Chandler. Their Stax hit was 1972's "Starting All Over Again."

~ *Soul Deep*

Like Little Richard before him, Otis Redding grew up in Macon, Georgia. He began as a member of the Pinetoppers, then the Shooters, before releasing his first solo hit, 1963's "These Arms of Mine." Besides being a fine soul singer, Redding was also an exceptionally good writer; he wrote or cowrote "I've Been Loving You Too Long (to Stop Now)," "Respect," "Try a Little Tenderness" and "(Sittin' on) the Dock of the Bay" (1965-67). Redding also had hits with Carla Thomas: "Tramp," "Knock on Wood" and "Lovey Dovey" (1967-68). The Bar-Kays (5) recorded and toured with Redding frequently. Their biggest hit was 1967's "Soul Finger." Both Otis and the Bar-Kays were surely destined for even greater success when on December 10, 1967, their chartered plane crashed into icy Lake Monona, Wisconsin. Redding and Bar-Kays Jimmy King, Ron Caldwell, Phalin Jones and Carl Cunningham died. The two surviving members re-formed the group. Redding's "Dock of the Bay" went to Number One in early 1968.

4

5

1

2

3

❧ *Soul Deep*

Arthur Alexander (4) was working as a bellhop when he recorded "You Better Move On" in 1961. It became the first hit recorded at Rick Hall's famed Muscle Shoals studio, and was followed by "Where Have You Been (All My Life)" and "Anna (Go to Him)," later covered by the Beatles. Clarence Carter (1), formerly a member of a group that recorded at Muscle Shoals, had several solo hits, including "Slip Away," "Too Weak to Fight" (1968) and "Patches" (1970). O. V. Wright (5) wrote "That's How Strong My Love Is," a hit for Otis Redding, and had his own success with "Eight Men, Four Women" (1967) and "Ace of Spades" (1970). Cousins James and Bobby Purify (3) scored with their first release, 1966's "I'm Your Puppet." Later hits included "Let Love Come between Us" and "Shake a Tail Feather" (1967). James Carr's (6) short run of hits included "Love Attack," "Pouring Water on a Drowning Man" and "The Dark End of the Street" (1966-67). Jimmy Hughes's (2) two best-known releases were "Steal Away" (1964) and "Neighbor, Neighbor" (1966).

4

5

6

✒ *Star Dust*

Having the ability to sing seemed to
present neither a help nor a
hindrance to the many television
and film stars who continued to cut
records. In 1962, two TV MDs
released their singing debuts.
Richard Chamberlain's (1) "Theme
from Dr. Kildare" went Top Ten,
while Vincent (Ben Casey)
Edwards's (5) "Why Did You Leave
Me" stalled in the sixties. Patty Duke
(3), who played two identical
cousins on *The Patty Duke Show*,
recorded "Don't Just Stand There"
in 1965. That year, comedian Soupy
Sales (6) launched a dance craze
with "The Mouse," a song that
featured King Curtis (right) on sax.
Years later, sex kitten Joey
Heatherton (2) covered Ferlin
Husky's "Gone," and Mae West (4)
did "Great Balls of Fire."

4

5

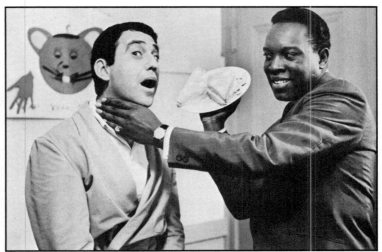

6

♪ *What Kind of Fool*

Because rock & roll is a music with no restrictions and few rules, anyone can make a record. Here's proof: Mrs. Elva Miller (2) was a tone-deaf grandmother with ambition. Her caterwauling renditions of "Downtown" and "A Lover's Concerto" were hits in 1966. Tiny Tim (5) became a national phenomenon in 1968 at the age of forty-three. Born Herbert Khaury, he sang '20s and '30s oldies, like "Tiptoe through the Tulips," in an exaggerated falsetto, accompanying himself on ukulele. Staff Sgt. Barry Sadler (1, with Ed Sullivan) was an ex-Green Beret who'd served in Vietnam. He had the Number One song of 1966, "The Ballad of the Green Berets." Chuck Barris (3), better known as the mastermind behind several TV game shows, recorded for Capitol Records and wrote Freddy Cannon's "Palisades Park." David Seville (4) (Ross Bagdasarian) was the man behind the Chipmunks. He had a flair for real music, having written "Come On-A My House" for Rosemary Clooney in 1951. Chipmunks Alvin, Simon and Theodore sang his Number One "The Chipmunk Song" in 1958.

3

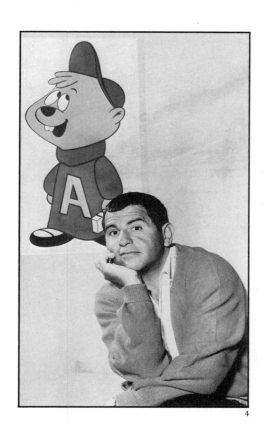

4

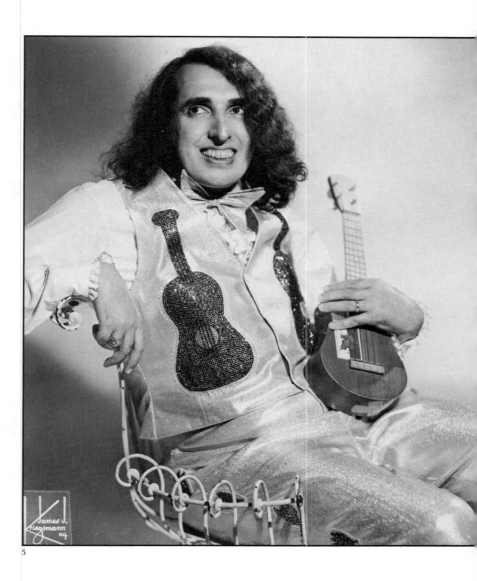

5

303

✑ *Blue on Blue*

Bobby Vinton (1), the Polish Prince, had a slew of MOR hits, including four Number Ones: "Roses Are Red" (1962), "Blue Velvet," "There! I've Said It Again" (1963) and "Mr. Lonely" (1964). Adam Wade's (2) hits were "As If I Didn't Know," "Take Good Care of Her" and "The Writing on the Wall" (1961). Lenny Welch's (4) two biggest singles were "Since I Fell for You" (1963) and "You Don't Know Me" (1960). Wayne Newton's (7, right) relative lack of visibility on the charts—"Danke Schoen" (1963) and "Daddy Don't You Walk So Fast" (1972)—never hurt his status as one of Las Vegas's top-drawing performers. Singer/actress Barbra Streisand's (6) two biggest singles in the '60s were "People" (1964), from the musical *Funny Girl*, and Laura Nyro's "Stoney End" (1970). Chicana Vikki Carr (5) scored with several singles, including "It Must Be Him" (1967) and "With Pen in Hand" (1969). O. C. Smith's (3) 1968 Number Two hit was "Little Green Apples."

1

2

3

4

5

6

7

3   4   5

♫ *Teenager's Romance*

Johnny Tillotson (3) was a country singer before he recorded "Without You," "Poetry in Motion" and "It Keeps Right On A-Hurtin'" (1960-62). Brian Hyland (5) was sixteen when he cut his 1960 Number One novelty, "Itsy Bitsy Teenie Weenie Yellow Polkadot Bikini." In 1962, Hyland went Top Ten with "Sealed with a Kiss." Bobby Goldsboro (4) had backed up Roy Orbison on guitar before starting a solo career with "See the Funny Little Clown" in 1964. Four years later, Goldsboro was a household name thanks to his million-selling ode to a dead bride, "Honey." Johnny Restivo (6) had the appropriately titled "The Shape I'm In" (1959). Of all the '60s teen rockers, none was as consistent as Tommy Roe (1, 2). From 1962, when his "Sheila" went to Number One, until 1971, Roe had several hits, including "Everybody," "Sweet Pea," "Hooray for Hazel" and "Dizzy."

6

5

6

♪ *Midnight Hours*

In 1966, Howard Tate (4) released
two hits, "Ain't Nobody Home,"
followed by "Get It While You Can."
That same year, Percy Sledge's (1)
classic "When a Man Loves a
Woman" went to Number One. In
1968, Sledge returned with "Take
Time to Know Her." Joe Simon (2)
had Top Twenty hits with "The
Chokin' Kind," "Drowning in the Sea
of Love" and "Get Down, Get Down"
(1969-75). The premier black female
vocalist of the '60s was Lady Soul,
Aretha Franklin (5, 6). She began
singing as a child in her father's
Baptist church. At Atlantic Records,
she released fourteen Top Ten
songs, including "I Never Loved a
Man," "Respect," "Baby I Love You,"
"A Natural Woman" and "Chain of
Fools" (1967-68). Her sister Erma (3)
recorded the original version of
"Piece of My Heart" in 1967, the
same year that Janis Joplin and Big
Brother and the Holding Company
made it a hit.

309

∿ *Midnight Hours*

Born into a family of gospel singers, Dionne Warwick (2, 3) began performing with the Drinkard Singers, a group that included her sister Dee Dee (1) and their aunt Cissy Houston (later of the Sweet Inspirations). In 1962, she began recording Burt Bacharach–Hal David songs, and charted many hits, including "Anyone Who Had a Heart," "Walk On By," "Message to Michael," "I Say a Little Prayer," "(Theme from) Valley of the Dolls" and "I'll Never Fall in Love Again" (1963-69). After several dry years, she returned with "Then Came You" (with the Spinners), "Déjà Vu" and "Heartbreaker" (1974-82). Dee Dee recorded "I Want to Be with You" (1966). Wilson Pickett (4, 5) sang with the Violinaires and the Falcons before embarking on a solo career that yielded "In the Midnight Hour," "634-5789 (Soulsville, U.S.A.)," "Land of 1000 Dances," "Mustang Sally," "Funky Broadway," "Hey Jude" and "Don't Knock My Love—Pt. 1" (1965-71).

4

5

↜ *Midnight Hours*

The Soul Clan—Otis Redding, Don Covay, Joe Tex, Solomon Burke and Ben E. King—planned to record together. Redding died and his protégé Arthur Conley (1) (whose 1967 hit, "Sweet Soul Music," Redding had produced) took his place. The Soul Clan's only releases were "Soul Meeting" and "That's How I Feel" (1968). Ben E. King's (4) post-Drifters hits included "Spanish Harlem," "Stand by Me" (1961), "Don't Play That Song" (1962) and "I (Who Have Nothing)" (1963). Solomon Burke (3) had hits with "Just Out of Reach" (1961), "Cry to Me" (1962) and "Got to Get You off My Mind" (1965). Don Covay, here with producer Jerry Wexler (2, right), recorded the 1964 single "Mercy, Mercy," later covered by the Rolling Stones. Joe Tex's (5) bawdy, humorous tunes included "Hold What You've Got" (1965), "Skinny Legs and All" (1967) and "I Gotcha" (1972). Tex died of a heart attack in 1982 at age forty-nine. Wilson Pickett, King and Covay were among his pallbearers.

1

3

5

4

2

♫ *Summer in the City*

Jay (David) Black and the Americans (2) had several Top Ten hits, including "She Cried," "Only in America," "Come a Little Bit Closer," "Cara Mia" and "This Magic Moment" (1962-67). During the early '70s Steely Dan's Donald Fagen and Walter Becker were part of their tour band. The Tokens (5) worked briefly as Neil Sedaka's backup vocal group before recording the Number One "The Lion Sleeps Tonight," which was based on an African folk song. The Happenings' (6) biggest hit was 1966's "See You in September." In 1965, the Trade Winds (3) scored with "New York's a Lonely Town," followed the next year by "Mind Excursions." In 1967 the group recorded as Innocence. The Chartbusters' (4) two 1964 hits were "She's the One" and "Why (Doncha Be My Girl)." The Lafayettes (1) recorded "Life's Too Short" (1962).

6

315

∿ *Summer in the City*

The Four Seasons (1, 2), formed in 1956, is the most successful white doo-wop group ever. With lead singer Frankie Valli (3, left) and writer/producer Bob Gaudio (3, right), the Seasons had over twenty-five hits, among them these Number Ones: "Sherry," "Big Girls Don't Cry," "Walk like a Man" and "Rag Doll." Another top New York group, the Lovin' Spoonful (4, 5), formed in 1965 from musicians in Greenwich Village. Lead singer John Sebastian (6) wrote the group's biggest hits— "Do You Believe in Magic," "Daydream" and "Summer in the City" (1965-66), and scored a few movies. The Spoonful's homespun, happy-go-lucky image and popularity were shattered when the press revealed that two members had set up the arrest of a drug dealer in exchange for immunity from prosecution on a marijuana-possession charge.

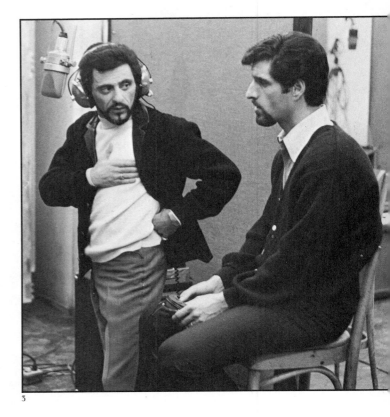

4

5

6

1

2

✒ *Summer in the City*

Three of the Rascals (1)—Gene
Cornish, Eddie Brigati (2) and Felix
Cavaliere—met while working as
some of Joey Dee's Starliters. With
drummer Dino Danelli, they formed
the Young Rascals. Their many hits
epitomized blue-eyed soul: "Good
Lovin'," "Groovin'," "How Can I Be
Sure," "A Beautiful Morning" and
"People Got to Be Free" (1966-68).
The Soul Survivors' (3) hits were
"Expressway to Your Heart" (1967)
and "Explosion in My Soul" (1968).
The Bronx-bred Blues Magoos (5)
hit with "(We Ain't Got) Nothin' Yet"
(1967). One member of Blue Eyed
Soul (4) was Billy Vera. Vanilla
Fudge (6) covered such current hits
as "You Keep Me Hangin' On."
Fudge's Carmine Appice and Tim
Bogert formed Cactus before
forming Beck, Bogert and Appice
with Jeff Beck.

3.

4.

5

6

319

1

2

3

4

5

🎵 *Summer in the City*

Though formed in L.A., composer/guitarist/arranger Frank Zappa's (1, lower right) Mothers of Invention moved to New York City in 1967. The Fugs (2), led by Ed Sanders and Tuli Kupferberg, satirized the flower-power generation. Velvet Underground (5), formed by avant-gardist John Cale and singer Lou Reed, was one of the first rock bands to celebrate the darker side of life. Discovered by Andy Warhol, who added German singer/keyboardist Nico (6), the Velvets focused on themes of drug addiction, death and sex. The Blues Project (3) became a key influence on the '60s blues revival. Arranger, songwriter, singer and keyboardist Al Kooper left the group to form the immensely popular Blood, Sweat and Tears (4). Their singles included one with Kooper ("I Can't Quit Her," 1967), and many hits with Canadian singer David Clayton-Thomas: "You've Made Me So Very Happy," "Spinning Wheel" and "And When I Die" (each of which hit Number Two in 1969).

6

❧ *Summer in the City*

Tommy James and the Shondells (5, 6) recorded fourteen top singles, ranging from bubblegum to basic psychedelia. Their hits included "Hanky Panky," "I Think We're Alone Now," "Mony Mony," "Crimson and Clover" and "Crystal Blue Persuasion" (1966-69). In 1971, James had a solo hit with "Draggin' the Line." The Strangeloves (2) were a studio group comprised of writer/producers Richard Gottehrer, Jerry Goldstein and Robert Feldman. Their hits were "I Want Candy" (1965) and "Night Time" (1966). The Knickerbockers (4), which included Royal Teen Buddy Randell, had two top singles, "Lies" and "One Track Mind" (1966). The Hassles (3) were Billy Joel's (left) first recording group ("You've Got Me Hummin'," 1967). In the group was Jonathan Small, with whom Joel later formed the duo Attila and whose wife, Elizabeth, later married —and managed—Joel. The Wind in the Willows was an early folk-rock band, notable now for the inclusion of singer Deborah Harry (1).

5

6

~✹ *Kick Out the Jams*

Detroit's strictly blue-collar rock made its influence felt when Mitch Ryder (7) and the Detroit Wheels (4) had their first hit, a medley of "Jenny Jenny" and "C.C. Rider" (1966). Later that year, they had a Top Five hit with "Devil with a Blue Dress On & Good Golly Miss Molly" (1966). Bob Seger (6, with his high-school band; Seger on knees in front) was a Michigan legend for more than a decade before finally breaking nationally in 1976 with *Live Bullet*. Terry Knight and the Pack (2) later evolved into Grand Funk Railroad (1), a crude, loud band. Though not exactly the critics' favorite, they did sell out Shea Stadium in 1971 faster than the Beatles had little more than a half decade earlier. The MC5 (5) were the house band for John Sinclair's White Panthers. Eventually, they split with Sinclair and dropped the politics. The Stooges were led by Iggy Pop (3) (born James Osterberg), one of rock & roll's true eccentrics. Bent on self-destruction (literally, in Iggy's case), they produced five raw, primitive LPs that portended the punk era.

4

5

6

7

1

2

❧ Kick Out the Jams

Groups to emerge from Chicago included Spanky (Elaine McFarlane) (3, second from left) and Our Gang, who had the Top Twenties "Sunday Will Never Be the Same," "Lazy Day" and "Like to Get to Know You" (1967-68). The Buckinghams (4) recorded "Kind of a Drag," "Don't You Care" and "Mercy, Mercy, Mercy" (1966-67), and the American Breed (1) did "Bend Me, Shape Me" in 1967. From Ohio came the Outsiders (5) with "Time Won't Let Me" in 1966. Another Chicago band, the Shadows of Knight (6) first hit with "Gloria" and "Oh Yeah" in 1966. The Ohio Express (2) was a leading Kasenetz-Katz/Buddah bubblegum band whose hits included "Yummy, Yummy, Yummy" and "Chewy Chewy" (1968). The Cryan' Shames (7) did "Sugar and Spice" in 1966.

3

5

4

6

7

1

2

3

〰 *North of the Border*

From Canada came Levon (Helm) (4, far right) and the Hawks, who had evolved from Canadian-based rockabilly Ronnie Hawkins's group. Helm, Richard Manuel, Rick Danko, Robbie Robertson and Garth Hudson moved to Greenwich Village, where Bob Dylan made them his backup band. They (minus Helm) toured with Dylan until his 1966 motorcycle crash, at which time Helm rejoined. The Band (5) woodshedded in West Saugerties, near Woodstock, and in 1968 released *Music from Big Pink*. Their chart singles include "The Weight," "Up on Cripple Creek" "Rag Mama Rag," and "Don't Do It" (1969-72). The Guess Who's (3) roots go back to 1963 when Chad Allan and Randy Bachman founded the group. Their first U.S. hit was 1965's "Shakin' All Over." Their next hits featured lead vocalist Burton Cummings: "These Eyes," "Laughing," "No Time," "American Woman" and "Share the Land" (1969-70). Also pictured here, a Canadian show band called Mandala (1) and the Beau Marks (2) ("Clap Your Hands").

4

5

1

2

3

〰️ *South of the Border*

The McCoys (2)—brothers Rick and
Randy Zehringer and a bass-playing
friend—had three big hits, "Hang On
Sloopy," "Fever" and "Come On,
Let's Go" (1965-66). By then, Rick's
surname was Derringer, and within
a few years, he'd joined the Johnny
Winter Band and then Winter's
brother Edgar's White Trash. Ocala,
Florida's Royal Guardsmen (5) had
several hits, the biggest of which
were inspired by a comic strip:
"Snoopy versus the Red Baron" and
"The Return of the Red Baron"
(1966-67). The Classics IV (3), with
lead singer Dennis Yost, recorded
"Spooky," "Stormy" and "Traces"
(1968-69). Members Buddy Buie and
J. R. Cobb later cofounded the
Atlanta Rhythm Section. Another
member of both bands, Dean
Daughtry, was a member of Atlanta's
Candymen (6), who released 1967's
"Georgia Pines"; the Music
Explosion (4) hit with "Little Bit o'
Soul," also in 1967. The Hourglass
(1) included brothers Duane (bottom
left) and Gregg Allman (middle).

1

2

3

❧ *South of the Border*

In 1965, the Uniques (3), with Joe Stampley (middle), had a minor hit with "Not Too Long Ago." That same year, the Ron-Dels (7)—Ronnie Kelly (left) and Delbert McClinton (right) —barely grazed the charts with "If You Really Want Me To, I'll Go." John Fred, here (2, left to right) with Robert Parker of "Barefootin'" fame and band member Ronnie Goodson, recorded fifteen records before he and his Playboy Band zoomed to Number One with "Judy in Disguise (with Glasses)" in 1967. The Newbeats (6) had three Top Twenty hits, "Bread and Butter," "Everything's Alright" (1964) and "Run, Baby, Run" (1965). The Five Americans (4) had hits with "I See the Light" (1966) and "Western Union" (1967). The New Colony Six (1) charted several singles from 1967 to 1971; their biggest was "Things I'd Like to Say" (1969). Mouse, who fronted the Traps (5), did "Public Execution," a cult hit in 1966.

4

5

6

7

❧ *Dirty Water*

If Frisco could have a scene, so could Boston. Or so reasoned MGM Records, who christened the city's groups part of the "Bosstown Sound" in 1968. The bands flopped dismally. Their names were intriguing, e.g., Ultimate Spinach (2) and the Beacon Street Union (1). Their music was not as noteworthy as their names. Orpheus (3) managed to score with a pretty pop ballad, "Can't Find the Time." The one Beantown act that *should* have made it, but didn't, was the Remains (4), led by Barry Tashian, currently a member of Emmylou Harris's band. Chain Reaction (5) never made it as a band, but their drummer, Steve Tyler (right), later became the lead singer for Aerosmith. Before the "Bosstown Sound" declaration, there were the Barbarians (6), whose one-handed drummer was the singer and subject of the '66 nugget "Moulty."

1

2

3

1

❧ *Are You Sure Hank Done It This Way?*

One of the biggest pop country stars was Roger Miller (1). In 1964 he went Top Ten with "Dang Me," followed by "King of the Road" (1965) and others. In 1969 Roy Clark (2) became known as one of the stars of *Hee Haw*, and that same year he had his biggest pop hit with "Yesterday, When I Was Young" (1969). Jerry Reed (4), the Alabama Wildman, recorded the original versions of "U.S. Male" and "Guitar Man" in the late '60s. His "Tupelo Mississippi Flash" is a song he wrote about Elvis. Singing journalist Tom T. Hall (5) wrote Jeannie C. Riley's "Harper Valley P.T.A." His own hits include "I Love" (1973). Sausage King Jimmy Dean (3) (Seth Ward) began recording in 1953. His two giant hits were the Number One "Big Bad John" (1961) and "PT 109" (1962), a tribute to John F. Kennedy's World War II exploits. Dean also hosted an early-'60s TV variety program.

1

2

♪ *Are You Sure Hank Done It This Way?*

George Jones (4, left), the greatest country singer of all time, hit in 1956 with "Why, Baby, Why," followed by "She Thinks I Still Care" (1962), "The Race Is On" (1964) and countless other hits. He later recorded with Gene Pitney and Elvis Costello, among others. In 1969 he married Tammy Wynette (5), whose top singles included "Stand by Your Man" (1968), "D I V O R C E" (1969) and several duets with Jones, whom she divorced in 1975. Johnny Paycheck's (1) first hit was 1966's "The Loving Machine," but his biggest was "Take This Job and Shove It." Between 1963 and 1972 alone Buck Owens (3) had 25 consecutive Top Ten country hits, including "Together Again" (1964) and "Waiting in Your Welfare Line" (1966). Dottie West (6) had such top singles as "Would You Hold It against Me" (1966) and "Country Sunshine" (1973). Claude King (2) is best known for 1962's "Wolverton Mountain."

3

4

5

6

♪ *Are You Sure Hank Done It This Way?*

Waylon Jennings (2) had been a
teenage disc jockey before he joined
Buddy Holly as bassist on his last
tour in 1959. Holly produced
Jennings's first single, "Jolé Blon."
Following years of touring and
recording, Jennings broke big after
teaming up with Willie Nelson (5)
for 1976's *Wanted: The Outlaws*.
Nelson had written "Crazy," "Night
Life," "Hello Walls" and "Ain't It
Funny How Time Slips Away." His
own solo career didn't take off until
1975's "Blue Eyes Crying in the
Rain" and 1976's "Good Hearted
Woman." Porter Wagoner and Dolly
Parton (4) had several duet hits
("Just Someone I Used to Know,"
1969; "Daddy Was an Old Time
Preacher Man," 1970) before Parton
went solo in 1974 and crossed over
four years after that with "Here You
Come Again." She later recorded
"Higher and Higher," "Two Doors
Down," "Baby I'm Burning" and
"9 to 5." Loretta Lynn (6) has
become a country legend through
her autobiography and the film it
inspired, *Coal Miner's Daughter*.
Sandy Posey (3) recorded "Born a
Woman" and "Single Girl" (1966).
Merle Haggard (1) is the working-
man's singer. His best songs include
"Mama Tried."

5

6

341

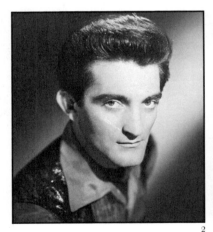

⌇ *Are You Sure Hank Done It This Way?*

Recording artist Mickey Newbury (3) is known primarily for writing such songs as Jerry Lee Lewis's "She Even Woke Me Up to Say Goodbye" and Elvis's "American Trilogy." Jeannie C. Riley (6) had a Number One pop hit with 1968's "Harper Valley P.T.A." Nashville pianist Floyd Cramer's (5) biggest hit record was "Last Date" (1960). His piano licks have appeared on countless singles by everyone from Elvis to the Everlys. Cajun fiddle king Doug Kershaw (2) made his chart debut in 1961 with "Louisiana Man," which he recorded with his brother under the name Rusty and Doug; "Diggy Liggy Lo" followed. Hank Williams, Jr., (1) started recording while still a child. In the '70s, he finally escaped his father's legacy, and after almost being killed in a mountain-climbing accident, came back stronger than ever with many country hits. The Statler Brothers' (4) first pop hit was 1964's "Flowers on the Wall."

4

5

6

5

6

4

✺ *Good Vibrations*

Gary Lewis (4, middle) had not only
the benefit of a famous father—
comedian Jerry Lewis—but the
studio support of great sessionmen
(such as Leon Russell) and producer
Snuff Garrett. His first of many hits
was the Al Kooper-penned "This
Diamond Ring." The Safaris (1) had
a hit with the romantic ballad
"Image of a Girl." Kenny Rogers (7)
made his second big splash with the
First Edition, a group whose first hit
was "Just Dropped In (to See What
Condition My Condition Was In)."
They next moved into the country
direction Rogers would fully exploit
years later with "Ruby Don't Take
Your Love to Town." Harper's
Bizarre's (5) one smash was Paul
Simon's "59th Street Bridge Song
(Feelin' Groovy)." Singer Ted
Templeman later produced Van
Halen. Dante and the Evergreens'
(3) "Alley Oop" was a novelty hit in
1960. Barry and the Tamerlanes (2)
went Top Thirty with "I Wonder
What She's Doing Tonight." Don and
the Good Times (6) released "I
Could Be So Good to You" and
"Happy and Me" (1967).

7

1

2

✎ *Good Vibrations*

Mid-to-late-'60s L.A. presented a cornucopia of pop styles. The protopunk Syndicate of Sound (2) recorded "Little Girl." The Standells' (3) "Dirty Water" (1966) was updated more than a decade later by Britain's the Inmates. Nobody has to cover a Union Gap (4) hit in the '80s; lead singer Gary Puckett (second from left) still performs. Pat and Lolly Vegas (1) were American Indians who wrote P. J. Proby's "Niki Hoeky." They later formed their own all-Indian band, Redbone, and enjoyed several hits ("Witch Queen of New Orleans," "Come and Get Your Love") before fading. An L.A. legend in his teens, Emitt Rhodes's career never reached the point where it could fade—it never really happened. In the '60s, during his early teens, he was a member of both the Palace Guard (6) and the Merry Go Round (7) ("You're a Very Lovely Woman"). He also wrote and produced. Also pictured: Carp with future actor Gary Busey (5, left).

3

4

5

6

7

1

2

3

4

≈ *Good Vibrations*

Oregonians Paul Revere and the Raiders (5), with their Revolutionary War-era outfits, were a highly profitable hit machine from 1961 to 1971. Pony-tailed Mark Lindsay (bottom right) was one of the finest singers of the day. The Kingsmen (4), also from Oregon, recorded "Louie Louie" (1963), its three-chord progression the basis for countless other tunes. Spirit (1), formed in 1967, were the antithesis of a commercial act, their music incorporating elements of jazz, blues, country and rock. The Electric Prunes (6) strived to be equally adventurous in 1967, but

ended up as a pretentious failure (the bloated *Mass in F Minor*). They recorded the quintessential psychedelic nugget "I Had Too Much to Dream (Last Night)" (1967). Canned Heat (2) sought to return to basics with a spare but emotive blues sound highlighted by Alan "Blind Owl" Wilson's harp and hulking Bob "Bear" Hite's gravelly vocals. Wilson died in 1970; Hite, in 1981. Also pictured here is the legendary Seattle garage band, the Sonics (3).

∿ *Good Vibrations*

The Monkees (1, 2, 3) took a lot of abuse for being a Beatles carbon copy, manufactured for Don Kirshner's TV show. The four did not play on their early records, although Peter Tork had drifted around L.A. as a folkie and Mike Nesmith was a talented singer/songwriter. Britisher Davy Jones and drummer/vocalist Mickey Dolenz were actors. Eventually the band was able to play its instruments capably and toured. Satisfied with their string of hits ("Last Train to Clarksville," "I'm a Believer") but frustrated by their one-dimensional image, Tork—and later Nesmith—quit. Sonny and Cher (4, 5) were a couple whose singing career took off with 1965's Number One "I Got You Babe." They had a popular Vegas act and a prime-time television series before they went their separate ways in the early '70s. Sonny wrote or cowrote many of their hits. Mott the Hoople covered his "Laugh at Me."

4

5

2

1

3

4

5

❦ *Good Vibrations*

The Count 5 (5), whose Yardbirds-inspired "Psychotic Reaction" hit in 1966, were famous for their capes. Iron Butterfly's (3) oxymoronic name was typical of the era. Their *In-A-Gadda-Da-Vida* was one of Atlantic Records' biggest sellers. Strawberry Alarm Clock (6) were one of the last psychedelic groups, with their laughable "Arabian" getups and hit single "Incense and Peppermints." Steppenwolf (4) was formed in 1967 by John Kay (1), after he left the Canadian group Sparrow. They had several chart successes, but none so influential as their motorcycle anthem "Born to Be Wild" (1968). The Chambers Brothers (2) continue to perform. The four Mississippi-born brothers moved to L.A. in the late '50s and eventually combined their gospel singing with rock instrumentation. Their biggest hit was 1968's psychedelic classic "Time Has Come Today."

6

1

2

♪ *Good Vibrations*

L.A.'s underground bands explored
the collective psyche's darker side in
their lyrics, and the music mirrored
that. The Seeds (2) grew out of
leader Sky Saxon's first band, the
Amoeba (1), and recorded the classic
"Pushin' Too Hard." Love (3), guided
by Arthur Lee, one of the few black
rockers, were even more ambitious,
writing suite-like compositions,
such as the twenty-minute
"Revelation." Jim Morrison (5) and
the Doors (4) were perhaps the best
creators of lengthy pieces ("The
End" and "When the Music's Over").
Other hits included "People Are
Strange," "Hello, I Love You,"
"Touch Me" and "Love Her Madly."
Their name came from an Aldous
Huxley book, *Doors of Perception*,
and vocalist Morrison was a poet
himself—several of the quartet's
songs included spoken-word
segments. Morrison, son of a naval
officer, was famous for his lack of
moderation, on and off stage. That,
contends keyboardist Ray Manzarek,
today a successful producer, is what
eventually killed him at age twenty-
seven in July 1971.

3

4

5

~ *Israelites*

Johnny Nash (1) hailed from Houston and appeared regularly on Arthur Godfrey's TV show from 1956 to 1963. He had several teen hits, including 1959's "The Teen Commandments" with Paul Anka and George Hamilton IV. In the late '60s, he began recording at Byron Lee's Jamaica studios. The results included "Hold Me Tight" (1968) and "I Can See Clearly Now" (1972). Millie Small (3) had two ska/ protoreggae hits in 1964, "My Boy Lollipop" and "Sweet William." Prince Buster's (4) 1964 "Judge Dread" was rock-steady. The same year, he released "Ten Commandments of Man." Jackie Edwards (6), who'd written "Keep On Running" for the Spencer Davis Group, had a hit of his own, 1968's "Put Your Tears Away." In 1963 Desmond Dekker (5) and his group the Aces hit Number One in Jamaica with "Honor Thy Father and Mother." Six years later, "The Israelites" went Top Ten in the United States. One of the biggest reggae stars is Jimmy Cliff (2), who starred in *The Harder They Come* and whose hits include "Wonderful World, Beautiful People" and "Many Rivers to Cross" (1969).

1

2

3

5

4

6

1

2

3

♪ *Glad All Over*

It was skiffle music that got kids to pick up guitars, and the King of Skiffle was Scotsman Lonnie Donegan (7), whose 1956 hit was "Rock Island Line." Appreciation clubs sprang up all over the country, and many later rock stars, like George Harrison and Adam Faith, were Donegan fans. Cliff Richard (3) started playing skiffle before he was groomed as a more rocking kind of teen idol. Without a doubt, Richard—though clean-cut and polite—is the closest thing in Britain to Elvis, with over seventy-five hits from 1959 to the present ("Move It," "Living Doll," "Because They're Young"). But he didn't have his first U.S. Top Ten until 1976, with "Devil Woman." Frank Ifield's (6) two 1962 hits were "I Remember You" and "Lovesick Blues." Ian Whitcomb (1), noted pop musicologist and author, had a 1965 smash with the widely banned "You Turn Me On." Jonathan King (2), later the founder of U.K. Records, also had a 1965 hit, "Everyone's Gone to the Moon." And Donovan (4) was the era's reigning flower-power apostle. His hits included "Catch the Wind," "Sunshine Superman," "Mellow Yellow," "Hurdy Gurdy Man" and "Atlantis" (1965-69). Here with Dick Clark (5).

4

6

7

5

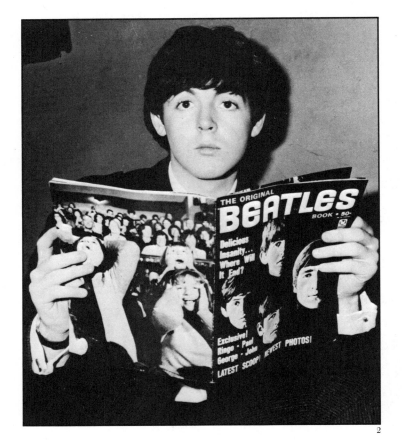

4

❧ *Glad All Over*

The Beatles changed rock & roll more than any artist before or after them. They introduced to the form new chord and harmonic structures, and, more significantly, altered the popular perception of the pop group—writing their own songs and functioning as a democracy, although it was John Lennon and Paul McCartney who most profoundly guided the quartet. Even though their early songs were relatively simple, they possessed a musical and lyrical sophistication rare in the typical pop fare of the day. In 1964, the year they conquered the United States, the Beatles at one point owned the Top Five singles on the Hot 100. But Beatlemania frustrated the Beatles, leading them to quit the road in 1966 and concentrate on recording. This was where their true genius evidenced itself, especially on the landmark *Sgt. Pepper's Lonely Hearts Club Band* (1967). The four broke up—acrimoniously—in 1970. Here with publicist Derek Taylor (middle) receiving their first gold record from Vee-Jay Records President Randy Wood (5).

5

4

5

≈ *Glad All Over*

The Dave Clark Five (1, 2) were
always more pragmatic than
romantic about rock & roll: They
originally formed to raise money for
their Tottenham Hotspurs soccer
team. But their singles—"Glad All
Over" and "Bits and Pieces"—were
driving rock & roll, powered by
drummer Clark. Two of the
Searchers' (3) original members are
still in the band, even though the
Searchers' last U.S. Top Ten hit was
1965's "Love Potion No. 9." The
influence of the Honeycombs, the
Swinging Blue Jeans and the
Zombies (6) was not so long-lasting.
The latter was the most successful,
racking up three U.S. hits, the last of
which, "Time of the Season," hit
Number Three after Rod Argent and
Company had gone their separate
ways. The Honeycombs (4) had one
huge chart success, "Have I the
Right?" and featured the rare
spectacle of a female drummer, Ann
"Honey" Lantree. The Swinging
Blue Jeans (5), with future Hollie
Terry Sylvester, recorded "Hippy
Hippy Shake" (1964).

6

1

2

〜 *Glad All Over*

To Americans, British Invasion bands seemed not unlike the Beatles, with long hair, tight trousers and electric guitars. But there was a *huge* difference between the Beatles and the Rolling Stones. While most British acts aped the styles of mainstream American rock & rollers, the Stones looked to the blues and R&B artists like Muddy Waters and Bo Diddley. And, unlike the Fab Four, who let their manager tidy them up, the Stones presented themselves as working-class louts. Eventually, singer Mick Jagger and guitarist Keith Richards began writing, and the Stones enjoyed many hits, beginning with 1965's "Satisfaction." Charter member Brian Jones (1, with Bob Dylan), who'd sparked the band's late-'60s eclecticism, died in 1969, sending the group back to the basics—and spurring it on to its "World's Greatest Rock & Roll Band" status. The Stones' creativity sagged in the mid-'70s, but Britain's punk explosion presented a challenge that the Stones accepted and—as 1978's *Some Girls* attests—met.

3

5

4

⌐⌐ *Glad All Over*

Most British acts circa 1964 were emulating the Beatles, with two notable exceptions. For the Kinks (4, 5), anchored by brothers Ray and Dave Davies, rock & roll presented an outlet for their anger—musically, in the pre-heavy metal of "You Really Got Me," and lyrically, in Ray's brooding, introspective statements about British life. Davies remains one of music's great wits and great showmen. The Animals (1, 3) may have come from Newcastle, but sounded as if they had been individually conceived in the bordellos of New Orleans, especially singer Eric Burdon (1, second from left), the blackest of the Limey vocalists. Originally called the Alan Price Combo after their keyboardist, the Animals recorded ten Top Twenty singles. Price left in 1965, and founded the Alan Price Set (2). The Animals then fell under the leadership of Burdon, who later recorded with War; their hit was 1970's "Spill the Wine."

1

2

3

4

5

6

7

✒ *Glad All Over*

The Nashville Teens' (2) sole hit was 1964's "Tobacco Road," and the Australian Easybeats (3) went Top Twenty in 1967 with "Friday on My Mind." The Fortunes (4) had three hits, "You've Got Your Troubles," "Here It Comes Again" (1965) and "Here Comes That Rainy Day Feeling Again" (1971). Wayne Fontana and the Mindbenders (1) had the 1965 Number One "Game of Love," and minus Fontana, "A Groovy Kind of Love" in 1966. Billy J. Kramer (5) and the Dakotas had two Top Tens: "Bad to Me" and "Little Children" (1964). With cofounder Graham Nash, the Hollies (6, 7) recorded "Just One Look," "Bus Stop" and "Carrie-Anne" (1964-67). Nash left in 1968, and the Hollies went on to greater success with "He Ain't Heavy, He's My Brother," "Long Cool Woman (in a Black Dress)" and "The Air That I Breathe" (1969-74).

5

6

⌇ *Glad All Over*

Lead singer Peter Noone was seventeen when his group, Herman's Hermits (5, 6), hit in late 1964 with "I'm into Something Good." Their later hits included "Can't You Hear My Heart Beat," "Mrs. Brown, You've Got a Lovely Daughter" and "I'm Henry VIII, I Am" (1965). Gerry (Marsden) and the Pacemakers (1) began performing around Liverpool in 1959. Their hits were "Don't Let the Sun Catch You Crying," "How Do You Do It?" and "Ferry Cross the Mersey" (1964-65). Freddie and the Dreamers (4, with Mike Douglas) recorded the Number One "I'm Telling You Now" and "Do the Freddie" (1965). Brian Poole and the Tremeloes (3) had a pair of 1967 hits, "Here Comes My Baby" and "Silence Is Golden." Unit Four Plus Two's (2) 1965 best-known single was "Concrete and Clay."

2

~ **Glad All Over**

The Bee Gees' (1, 3) career is actually the longest of any British Invasion group. The three Gibb brothers—Barry, Robin and Maurice —began performing together in 1955. In 1967, they had four Top Twenty hits, all featuring lush orchestration and very British harmonies. Maurice married U.K. songstress Lulu (2). The Bee Gees' sound was outdated by 1973, but they engineered a startling turnaround in 1975, and their contributions to the *Saturday Night Fever* soundtrack were largely responsible for the 30 million copies it sold. Peter (Asher) and Gordon (Waller) (4, 6) met in school and later had hits with "A World without Love" (1964), "I Go to Pieces" (1965) and "Lady Godiva" (1966). Asher is now a successful manager and producer. Chad (Stewart) and Jeremy (Clyde) (5) had two big 1964 hits, "Yesterday's Gone" and "A Summer Song."

4

5

6

⌇ *Two Faces Have I*

The British sound was selling, so many American acts adopted it. The Walker Brothers (1) not only weren't English, but weren't even brothers. Scott Engel, Gary Leeds and John Maus did move to England in 1964, however, and hit with "Make It Easy on Yourself" (1965) and "The Sun Ain't Gonna Shine Anymore" (1966). On "Laugh, Laugh," the Beau Brummels (2) sounded like they were from Liverpool, not San Francisco. Sir Doug Sahm's (3, left) first hit, "She's About a Mover," gave little evidence that the leader of the Sir Douglas Quintet hailed from Texas. Jimi Hendrix (4, 5), who changed the nature of the electric guitar like no one before or after him, moved from New York to London to establish his solo career. When he made jaws drop at the 1967 Monterey Pop Festival, many assumed he was British. Hendrix eventually grew frustrated by his role as black guitar-voodoo warrior; at the time of his September 1970 death, he was moving in a jazz-rock fusion direction. Here (left) with the Curtis Knight Group (6).

5

6

7

1

ᕁ *Rave Up*

Though the Yardbirds (1, 2, 3) were together but a short while, their influence on rock & roll— particularly guitar playing—was enormous. Founders Keith Relf, Chris Dreja, Paul Samwell-Smith and Jim McCarty stayed on while the group's lead guitarists were Eric Clapton, Jeff Beck and Jimmy Page. The Yardbirds' hits included "For Your Love" (1965), "Shape of Things" and "Over Under Sideways Down" (1966). The Who (4, 5, 6) were the leading exponents of the Mod movement. Leader/guitarist Pete Townshend and drummer Keith Moon built the band's reputation in part on their climactic destruction of their equipment at the end of each show. Their early hits included "I Can't Explain" (1965), "My Generation" (1966) and "I Can See for Miles" (1967).

2

4

5

6

Ro

Them (S
for Belfa
middle)
for their
Morrison
Comes t
produce
Pretty T
their En
The Tro
Thing,"
once cal
anthem
Manfred
bespect
Mann w
bust up
U.S. cha
"Do Wa
original
vocalist
hit, "Go
after La
Wings—
substan

2

1

3

5

6

1

✺ *Rave Up*

Cream (1) expanded the traditional
boundaries of the pop group into a
triumvirate in which the bass and
drums (Jack Bruce, second from left,
and Ginger Baker, second from
right) joined the guitar (Eric
Clapton, 2) as a lead instrument.
The trio sold over 15 million records
in its career, but after just two years,
Cream soured. Procol Harum (3)
were forerunners of classical rock.
Their first hit, "A Whiter Shade of
Pale," combined surreal lyrics with
an organ line taken directly from
Bach's Suite No. 3 in D major. Keith
Emerson's the Nice (5) also
combined classical melodies with
rock bombast, and they recorded
with an orchestra. Fleetwood Mac
(6), their moniker taken from the
combined surnames of drummer
Mick Fleetwood and bassist John
McVie, were part of the vanguard of
the 1967/1968 blues revival.
Fleetwood and McVie remain, but
the blues direction has been
replaced by cool California soft rock.
The rest of the European invasion
consisted of Spain's Los Bravos (4),
with "Black Is Black" in 1966.

2

3

4

6

5

1

✌ *Bits and Pieces*

The Spencer Davis Group (4), with
lead singer Steve Winwood, had two
big U.S. hits, "Gimme Some Lovin'"
and "I'm a Man" (1967), before
Winwood left to found Traffic (5).
With Dave Mason (6), Jim Capaldi,
Chris Wood and Winwood, Traffic's
best-known singles are 1967's
"Paper Sun" and "Mr. Fantasy." By
late 1968, Mason left for a solo
career. In 1969, Winwood founded
the supergroup Blind Faith (7).
Given the lineup—Winwood and
Ginger Baker, Eric Clapton and Rick
Grech—expectations were high.
Their popular tunes included "Can't
Find My Way Home" and "In the
Presence of the Lord." Silkie (1)
recorded the Beatles' "You've Got to
Hide Your Love Away" (1965). The
Seekers' (2) hits included "I'll Never
Find Another You" (1965) and
"Georgy Girl" (1966). Brian Auger
and the Trinity, with Julie Driscoll
(3), recorded for several years.
Among their songs is a cover of
Donovan's "Season of the Witch."

5

❧ *Bits and Pieces*

The Small Faces (5) were founded by singer Steve Marriott and had their biggest hit with "Itchycoo Park" in 1968. Marriott split in 1969; with the addition of Rod Stewart and Ron Wood, they became simply the Faces (6). Through 1975, Rod recorded both with and without them; their biggest hit was 1972's "Stay with Me." Roy Wood led the Move (4), a more eccentric kind of group whose popularity never crossed the Atlantic. In its later stages, the Move was joined by Jeff Lynne (2), who had earlier replaced Wood in a group called Idle Race (1).

In 1972, Lynne left to form the Electric Light Orchestra, whose many hits included a remake of the Move's "Do Ya." The Crazy World of Arthur Brown (3) had one tremendous smash—"Fire" (1968). Brown performed in a helmet, which when ignited gave the illusion that his hair was on fire. This was all the rage in London for a time, though never widely imitated.

6

⟿ *Bits and Pieces*

The British Invasion was generally commandeered by men. But in 1967, there was Lulu (5), a nineteen-year-old from Scotland, whose "To Sir with Love" hit Number One. She later married (and divorced) Bee Gee Maurice Gibb, went through a commercial dry spell, then returned to the charts in 1981. Mary Hopkin (2), from South Wales, was Paul McCartney's protégée; he produced her "Those Were the Days." Before Olivia Newton-John (3, left) became a superstar, she was in a duo with Pat Carroll, an Australian singer. Newton-John went C&W before finding her calling as a film star and balladeer. David Bowie (4) *was*

male, but there were times when gender appeared questionab... when Bowie wore a dress on... U.K. cover of *The Man Who S... World*. Van Morrison's (1) so... career kicked off with "Brow... Girl," but turned more spirit... his second album, *Astral We...* of the most haunting LPs of...

2

4

5

3

1

✒ *Get Together*

The disparities among the Grateful
Dead's (4) members typified the S.F.
scene's musical mélange. Guitarist
Jerry Garcia came from a folk and
bluegrass background, young Bob
Weir was a straight-out rocker,
Pigpen bummed the blues, and Phil
Lesh was an electronic-music
composer. Their collective sound
was rarely cohesive. Blue Cheer (2),
conversely, had one direction only.
This power trio plundered what
today would be termed heavy metal,
with their primitive update of Eddie
Cochran's "Summertime Blues."
Grace Slick and the Jefferson
Airplane (3) combined subversive
politics with a sound that varied
between folk and psychedelic.
Slick's cynicism informed such
songs as "Somebody to Love" and
"Lather," while partner/lover Paul
Kantner favored science-fiction
fantasy. By 1972, the Airplane
included David Freiberg, a founding
member of Quicksilver Messenger
Service (5). The Vejtables' (1) lone
charting single was "I Still Love
You" (1965).

4

5

1

✒ *Get Together*

Milwaukee-born Steve Miller migrated to San Francisco, where he put together the Steve Miller Blues Band (1) in 1966 with fellow itinerant Boz Scaggs, who joined in 1967. Unlike Miller, Moby Grape (4) suffered by the Frisco association and were marketed with the hype of the decade (eight simultaneously released 45s). The Chocolate Watch Band (2) are more memorable for their period-piece name than for their music ("Let's Talk about Girls"). Sly and the Family Stone—Sly (3) being ex-DJ/producer Sylvester Stewart—were one of rock's first multiracial acts. They featured frenetic vocal interplay and had three Number Ones, "Everyday People," "Family Affair" and "Thank You Faletinme Be Mice Elf Again." Creedence Clearwater Revival (5) voluntarily ended their career in 1972, capping four years as America's most prolific—and best—singles band. Since the breakup, talented leader John Fogerty has mostly stayed in seclusion.

~ *Get*

It was cal
Sound," b
encompa
blues to R
Janis Jopl
right), wit
Holding C
rooted in
intensifie
to be hear
deafening
went solo
of greater
died of an
overdose
Electric F
Bloomfiel
pioneered
blues-roc
the Fish (
politics w
Country J
Like-I'm-
Colin You
New York
where he
(4). In Sar
"Get Tog

2

394

3

4

5

6

PHOTO CREDITS

ABC/Paramount Records: 105/4, 118/2, 118/3, 159/5, 160/2, 161/5, 161/6, 165/6, 178/3, 217/6, 277/4, 306/1, 306/2, 331/6. Abnak Records: 333/4. Ace Records: 101/7, 101/8, 150/2, 150/3, 151/4. Paul Acree: 296/3, 297/4. Aladdin Records: 5/7, 120/3, 125/5. A&M Records: 347/6, 347/7, 356/2. The Apollo Theatre: 2/1, 4/3, 95/6. Apple Records: 389/2. Arctic Records: 263/5. Brooks Arthur: 187/5, 191/4, 196/1. Arvee Records: 181/3. Arwin Records: 246/1. Atlantic/Atco Records: 30/3, 31/4, 31/5, 66/1 (Popsie), 66/3 (Popsie), 98/3, 104/1, 112/2, 112/3, 113/6, 123/4, 148/2, 148/3, 149/4, 149/5, 216/2, 219/5, 263/7, 272/2, 275/6, 311/4, 312/2, 319/6, 328/1, 351/4, 351/5, 352/3, 372/2, 372/3, 380/1, 382/1, 384/3, 385/7, 386/3. Autumn Records: 574/2, 390/1. Bang Records: 284/3, 322/2 (Popsie). Bell Records: 286/3, 289/5, 346/2. Beltone Records: 253/3. Alan Betrock Collection: 52/1, 107/6, 223/6, 265/3, 333/7, 379/4, 386/1, 386/2, 387/6. Big Top Records: 195/5. John Blair: 59/4, 248/3. Blaze Records: 168/3. Blue Cat Records: 186/2. Blue Thumb Records: 554/3, 385/6. Harold Bronson (M.O.A.): 90/1, 209/5, 229/4, 321/6, 362/3 367/4, 367/5, 377/7, 580/2, 384/2, 386/4, 389/3, 389/4. Brunswick Records: 221/5. B.T. Puppy Records: 315/6. Cadence Records: 171/4. Cameo/Parkway Records: 81/6, 163/4, 163/5, 166/1, 166/2, 167/5, 180/1, 210/2, 324/2, 326/2. Canadian-American Records: 278/5. Bob Cain: 89/2. Capitol Records: 13/3, 15/5, 22/1, 22/2, 25/3, 28/3, 82/2, 108/1, 114/1, 114/2, 114/3, 115/4, 122/1, 140/2, 240/1, 240/2, 241/3, 242/2, 243/3, 243/4, 243/5, 243/6, 280/2, 283/5, 287/5 (Popsie), 302/2, 303/3, 305/7, 324/1, 327/5, 329/5, 337/2, 338/3, 340/1, 360/1, 360/2, 360/3, 373/4, 375/6, 577/6. Carlton Records: 106/1, 168/1. Ted Carroll: 152/1, 152/2, 137/5. Challenge Records: 158/4, 322/4. Chancellor Records: 162/2, 162/3, 164/1, 164/2, 164/3, 259/4, 267/5. Charger Records: 255/5. Chess Records: 7/3, 42/1 (Popsie), 42/2, 43/5, 43/6, 43/7, 44/1, 45/4, 45/5, 69/4, 73/4, 75/4, 79/5, 100/1, 102/2, 257/5, 258/3, 263/6, 277/5. Alan Clarke Collection: 117/3, 146/2, 154/1, 155/5, 155/6, 159/7, 172/2, 248/2, 249/4. Class Records: 110/2. Co-Ed Records (Popsie): 65/4. Paul Colby: 205/4. Colpix Records: 170/1, 171/8, 179/8. Columbia/Epic Records: x, 11/5, 12/1, 13/5, 13/6, 17/5, 47/4, 50/1, 50/2, 51/4, 56/2, 58/1, 59/3, 80/1, 82/1, 83/5, 87/4, 143/5, 147/6, 152/2, 152/3, 183/4 (Popsie), 206/1, 206/2, 245/5, 270/1, 271/3, 271/4, 271/5, 272/3, 283/5, 285/5, 304/1, 305/6, 309/5, 320/4, 327/4, 327/7, 355/4, 357/3, 337/4, 338/2, 343/4, 345/6, 346/1, 347/4, 347/5, 548/1, 349/5, 358/3, 359/5, 362/1, 370/3, 378/1, 378/3, 383/6, 389/5, 393/4. Combo Records: 37/5. Crest Records: 136/3, 281/6. Crimson Records: 319/3. Crusader Records: 106/4. Cub Records: 253/5. Dade Records: 253/5. Dakar Records: 214/2. Spencer Davis: 361/4, 385/4. Del-Fi Records: 136/4, 171/5. Del-Tone Records: 241/4. Demon Records: 175/2. Deram Records: 585/3. Detroit News: 220/3. Henry Diltz: 266/2, 266/3, 355/4, 359/4. Dimension Records (Popsie): 191/5. Dot Records: 10/1, 60/2, 69/3, 80/3, 81/5, 122/2, 145/4, 155/4, 299/4, 359/7. Double Shot Records: 254/1, 353/5. Duke/Peacock Records: 32/1, 32/2, 32/4, 33/5, 33/7, 33/8, 282/1. Dunes Records: 197/2, 197/3. Dunhill Records: 264/2, 265/4, 265/5, 352/4. Dunwich Records: 327/6. Dyno Voice Records: 325/4. Eldo Records: 344/1. Elektra Records: 324/3, 325/5. Ember Records: 79/4. Era Records: 62/2, 254/2, 258/1. Essex Records: 29/1. Jimmy Evans Management: 3/4. Excello Records: 68/2, 253/6. Fame Records: 298/1, 298/2 (Popsie). Narvel Felts: 61/5. Freddy Fender: 210/1. Fire/Fury Records: 121/4, 218/3. Flo & Eddie: 248/1. Fontana Records: 368/1, 384/1. Fraternity Records: 56/4, 333/5. Lance Freed: 38/2, 38/3, 39/6, 39/7. Ray Funk: 141/4. Ralph Gleason Collection (M.O.A.): 16/1, 119/4, 119/5. GNP Crescendo Records: 270/2, 354/2. Gold Chip Records:

554/1. Goldwax Records (Popsie): 299/6. Gone Records: 68/1, 107/8. Herb Green: 390/2, 391/4, 591/5, 392/1. Jonathan & Ronnie Greenfield: 198/1, 198/2, 199/3. Gregmark Records: 197/5. Peter Guralnick: 6/1, 7/2, 27/5, 106/3. Herald Records: 69/5, 176/2. Hi Records: 53/5, 289/3. Ersel Hickey: 51/5. Hickory Records: 353/6, 342/2. Richard Hite: 9/5, 9/6, 55/6. Bones Howe: 247/4, 269/4. Danny Hutton: 285/6. Immediate Records: 583/5, 387/5. Imperial Records: 93/3, 93/4, 95/7, 131/6, 154/2, 155/4, 254/4, 267/6, 330/3, 363/5, 368/5, 369/7. Instant Records: 94/2. Island: 357/6. JAD Records: 356/1. Jamie/Guyden Records: 146/1, 157/5, 188/2, 259/5. Jerden Records: 348/3. Josie Records: 174/1. Kama Sutra Records: 314/3, 317/4, 517/5, 317/6. Peter Kanze Collection (M.O.A.): 12/2, 19/4, 20/1, 24/1, 25/4, 25/5, 40/1, 41/3, 51/3, 88/1, 90/4, 91/5, 91/6, 162/1, 171/6, 183/3, 208/2, 215/4, 220/1, 224/1, 241/5, 260/3, 267/4, 268/3, 272/4, 277/6, 323/6, 325/6, 326/1, 328/3, 331/4, 331/5, 332/1, 332/2, 335/5, 337/5, 339/4, 340/4, 345/7, 373/5, 377/5, 378/2. Kent/Modern Records: 8/4, 110/3, 111/4. King/Federal Records: 8/1, 37/4, 56/1, 64/3, 74/2, 84/1, 84/2, 84/3, 85/4, 86/2, 87/5, 150/2. James Kriegsmann: 5/6, 10/2, 10/3, 10/4, 11/6, 13/4, 13/4, 16/2, 16/3, 17/6, 22/3, 28/1, 29/6, 30/1, 30/2, 34/1, 34/2, 35/3, 36/1, 36/2, 36/3, 44/2, 58/2, 60/3, 61/6, 64/1, 64/2, 65/5, 66/2, 66/4, 67/5, 67/6, 69/6, 70/1, 70/2, 70/3, 73/6, 75/3, 75/5, 77/2, 77/3, 78/1, 81/7, 83/4, 83/5, 90/2, 92/2, 95/5, 98/1, 99/4, 101/6, 103/5, 104/2, 104/3, 106/2, 108/2, 118/1, 122/3, 124/1, 125/3, 125/4, 128/3, 133/4, 135/4, 136/2, 140/1, 144/2, 145/5, 148/1, 150/1, 151/5, 158/2, 158/3, 159/6, 161/4, 165/5, 167/4, 167/6, 169/5, 176/1, 177/5, 177/6, 177/7, 178/1, 178/2, 180/2, 185/3, 185/4, 186/1, 187/4, 188/3, 189/5, 189/6, 190/1, 192/1, 193/5, 199/4, 200/3, 202/1, 202/2, 203/4, 203/5, 204/1, 204/2, 208/3, 212/4, 217/4, 217/5, 218/1, 220/2, 222/2, 225/5, 225/3, 225/4, 225/5, 226/2, 229/3, 229/5, 230/1, 234/2, 234/3, 235/5, 237/3, 237/4, 256/1, 256/2, 258/2, 259/6, 260/1, 260/2, 261/5, 261/6, 262/1, 262/2, 262/3, 263/4, 266/1, 279/5, 279/7, 294/2, 294/3, 294/4, 298/3, 299/5, 303/5, 304/3, 305/4, 307/3, 308/1, 308/5, 309/6, 310/1, 311/5, 312/1, 315/3, 314/5, 318/1, 528/2, 329/4, 330/2, 339/5, 395/6. Art Laboe: 89/4, 100/4, 141/5, 142/1, 147/5. Laurie Records: 128/1, 128/2, 129/4, 191/6, 370/1. Brenda Lee: 48/3, 127/4. Liberty Records: 62/3, 63/4, 116/1, 116/2, 145/6, 172/1, 173/3, 173/4, 173/5, 181/4, 192/2, 216/1, 246/2, 246/3, 247/5, 249/6, 251/4, 254/3, 280/1, 303/4, 305/5, 330/1, 348/2. Marshall Lieb: 197/4. London Records: 365/3, 565/5, 368/2, 370/2, 380/4. Love Records: 131/7. Madison Records: 344/3. MCA Records: 18/2, 20/3, 20/4, 23/4, 26/1, 29/4, 60/1, 62/1, 126/2, 127/6, 134/1, 134/2, 135/3, 136/1, 137/6, 244/2, 301/5, 341/6, 353/6, 557/5, 379/5, 379/6. Michael McGinnis: 205/3. Huey Meaux: 92/1, 146/3, 574/3. Arthur C. Mensor: 20/2, 48/1, 53/3. Mercury Records: 14/1, 28/2, 37/7, 76/1, 76/2, 80/2, 107/7, 136/1, 184/1, 190/2, 193/4, 193/6, 216/3, 244/1, 268/1, 274/1, 279/6, 283/4, 283/7, 526/3, 336/1, 357/5, 370/4, 374/1, 376/1, 376/2 (Popsie). Bob Merlis: 201/5. MGM/Verve Records: 18/3, 21/5, 26/2, 37/8, 106/5, 123/5, 126/1, 126/3, 127/5, 155/3, 175/4, 192/3, 209/4, 211/6, 250/1, 251/6, 284/2, 289/4, 300/1, 300/3, 308/4, 520/1, 320/3, 321/5, 334/1, 334/2, 334/3, 340/3, 342/1, 566/1, 366/3, 371/5, 371/6. Minit Records: 99/5, 100/2. Mira Records: 272/1. Money Records: 274/3. Monogram Records: 211/5. Monument Records: 195/3. Moonglow Records: 201/4. Motown Records: 222/1, 222/3, 222/4, 223/7 (Popsie), 224/2, 226/1, 226/3, 227/4, 227/5, 228/1, 250/3, 231/4, 232/1, 232/2, 233/3, 233/4, 233/5, 233/6, 234/1, 235/4, 236/1, 236/2, 237/3. Mutual Records: 314/4. New Town Records: 186/3. Nudie the Tailor: 49/5. Alice Ochs: 207/7, 318/2, 320/2, 325/7. Michael Ochs Archives: 95/3, 206/3, 210/3, 242/1, 268/2, 281/4, 288/1, 375/4, 375/5, 376/3, 581/5, 402.

Okeh Records: [...]
Records: 79/6, [...]
275/5. Jim O'N[...]
ords: 131/8, 179[...]
tion: 3/3, 9/7, [...]
111/5, 112/1, 112[...]
ords: 363/6, 36[...]
Don Paulsen: [...]
213/5, 228/2, 2[...]
316/2, 316/3, 31[...]
364/2, 365/4, 3[...]
394/1, 395/5. S[...]
L.A. of Soul Re[...]
200/1, 200/2. Pr[...]
ord Company: 5[...]
ords: 15/3, 18/1, [...]
46/1, 46/2, 47/3[...]
113/5, 125/6, 13[...]
153/3, 156/1, 15[...]
209/7, 245/3, 2[...]
341/5, 342/3, 34[...]
Red Bird Recor[...]
2/2, 3/5, 4/4, 7[...]
286/2, 349/6. [...]
286/1. Riversid[...]
71/5, 74/1, 80/4[...]
323/5. Rust Rec[...]
276/2. Sceptor [...]
Seville Records[...]
25/6, 95/4, 12[...]
166/3, 176/4, 1[...]
252/1, 252/2, 2[...]
307/4, 307/5, 3[...]
375/6. Dominic[...]
ter Sil: 156/4. S[...]
218/2, 343/6. So[...]
Records: 189/[...]
97/3, 97/4, 98/[...]
290/3, 291/2, 2[...]
292/4, 293/5, 2[...]
299/4. Steed [...]
203/6, 245/4. S[...]
55/5, 57/6, 131[...]
ords: 219/4. To[...]
301/4, 346/3, 3[...]
Records: 209/[...]
385/5. UK Reco[...]
guard Records[...]
72/2, 72/3, 73/[...]
251/5, 308/2, [...]
287/4. Billy Ve[...]
Vista Records[...]
348/4. Alan W[...]
56/3, 90/3, 170[...]
Warwick Rec[...]
207/5. White W[...]
man: 393/5, 39[...]

The photograp[...]
from many co[...]
permission of [...]
pictures as in [...]
produced with [...]
every attempt [...]
er owners, ho[...]
other photogra[...]
apologies to a[...]
be uncredited[...]
Michael Ochs [...]

INDEX

MICHAEL OCHS, rock & roll collector and historian, is considered one of the country's foremost rock archivists. He has been collecting and cataloging rock artifacts for almost two decades. During his long career in the music industry, he managed the career of his brother, singer/songwriter Phil Ochs, and later headed the public relations departments of Columbia, Shelter and ABC records. As a freelance writer, he contributed to such publications as *Rock*, the *L.A. Free Press*, *Melody Maker* and *Cashbox*, and he has written liner notes to a number of albums. This is his first book.

In the mid-'70s, Michael Ochs established the Michael Ochs Archives. Based in Venice, California, the Archives is a research service and library that contains one of the largest private collections of rock & roll, country, folk and jazz records in the country (over 100,000 albums and singles). It also contains the largest catalog of music photographs (over 100,000) and represents several photographers, including James J. Kriegsmann and Don Paulsen. The Archives also houses many photo collections, including those of Ralph J. Gleason and Peter Kanze. And the Archives contains an extensive library of rock-related books, periodicals and other pop memorabilia. The Archives has contributed to and provided photographs, props and/or music consultation for: movies (*Christine*, *Liar's Moon*, *The Rose*, *Hollywood Knights*, *This Is Elvis*, *The Chosen* and others), television programs (*The Heroes of Rock and Roll*, *Casey Kasem's America's Top Ten*, *When the Music's Over* and others), periodicals, repackaged record releases and books.

VINCENT WINTER has designed numerous books, including *Destinations* by Jan Morris (Rolling Stone Press/Oxford University Press), *The Rolling Stone Interviews* (Rolling Stone Press/St. Martin's Press) and *SpaceShots* by Timothy Ferris (Pantheon). *Destinations* was nominated for two American Book Awards for typography and design. He has also art directed several national magazines, including *Rolling Stone*, *Esquire* and *Inside Sports*. He currently designs books and magazine formats, and consults from his studio in New York City.

PETER GURALNICK is the author of *Lost Highway* (David R. Godine) and *Feel Like Going Home* (Vintage), two acclaimed works on popular music, and the novel *Nighthawk Blues* (Seaview), which portrays a fictional bluesman, the Screamin' Nighthawk. He contributed six chapters to *The Rolling Stone Illustrated History of Rock & Roll* (Rolling Stone Press/Random House), including a widely syndicated piece on Elvis Presley. He has written on blues, country & western and rockabilly music for *Rolling Stone*, the *New York Times Magazine*, the *Village Voice*, *Boston Phoenix*, *Living Blues* and *Country Music* magazine. He has just completed *Sweet Soul Music*, an account of Southern soul in the '60s, due to be published by Harper and Row in early 1985.

THIS BOOK was set by Mackenzie-Harris Corp. of San Francisco in Linotron Walbaum, a typeface originally designed between 1805 and 1828 in Germany by Justus Walbaum. The subheads were set in foundry Onyx. Ann Pomeroy hand-lettered the main title type.